GOLD

pre-first

exam maximiser with key

T0346029

Helen Chilton
Lynda Edwards

Introduction to the Gold Pre-First Exam Maximiser

The *Gold Pre-First Exam Maximiser* is designed to give you plenty of extra practice with the grammar, vocabulary and skills from the *Gold Pre-First Coursebook*. It will help you improve your language skills and maximise your chances of success when you come to sit the Cambridge English: First exam.

The *Exam Maximiser* will help you prepare for the Cambridge English: First exam. It provides:

- **practice and revision** of the important vocabulary, grammar and skills (reading, writing, listening, speaking) in the *Gold Pre-First Coursebook*.
- help with techniques you need for exam tasks and **exam-style activities** for you to practise these.
- a section on **useful language**.
- a complete **Practice test** to use before you take the Cambridge English: First exam.

What is in each unit?

The *Gold Pre-First Exam Maximiser* follows the structure of the *Gold Pre-First Coursebook*. Each unit provides more work on the language, skills and exam techniques you have studied in the Coursebook unit.

There are **Vocabulary** sections where you can practise the words and expressions you studied in the Coursebook. You'll also learn some new words and expressions. Activities include exam-style tasks as well as more fun activities like crosswords and wordsearch grids.

Each unit has two **Grammar** sections looking at the same points you studied in the Coursebook. There are activities to practise and revise the grammar and to help you identify where you might see it in the exam.

The **Speaking** sections include activities to help you build your abilities for the Speaking paper. There are activities working on useful language and on strategies for making yourself understood, agreeing and disagreeing and so on. Often, you listen to or read examples of candidates doing tasks and then complete activities to help your own speaking skills.

Every unit has a **Listening** section with an exam-style recording, so there's plenty of opportunity for you to practise your listening skills. As in the Coursebook, these tasks are based on the tasks you'll see in the exam and are designed to help you begin your preparation. Often, there's a section helping you with vocabulary from the text that you might not have seen before.

Similarly, the **Reading** section in each unit gives you more practice in dealing with the kinds of tasks you have covered in the Coursebook. You'll get some information about the exam and help with exam strategies and techniques. Like the Listening sections, many of the Reading sections have activities for you to practise unfamiliar words and phrases.

There is a **Writing** section in every unit of the *Exam Maximiser*. These sections will help you build skills you'll need for the exam, as well as for everyday writing tasks. You will be able to see examples of other people's writing and learn how to improve your own. In some tasks, you work on useful language or on planning and organising your writing, while in other tasks you write your own answers. You can check your written work against sample answers.

At the back of the book, there is a **Useful language** section, which includes language for important functions such as giving invitations, agreeing and disagreeing and making suggestions. There are also useful phrases for the Speaking and Writing papers.

After you have worked through all the units, you can try the **Practice test** at the back of the book. If you do this under timed exam conditions, it will give you a good idea of what to expect in the exam itself and your results will help you understand what to focus on as you prepare for it.

How can I use the Gold Pre-First Exam Maximiser?

You can use it with your teacher or on your own. Most of the time, you will write your answers to the activities in the *Exam Maximiser* itself. Most of the questions have only one answer, so they are very easy to correct. If you have an *Exam Maximiser* with a key, you can do the activities at home and correct them yourself. If you have an *Exam Maximiser* without a key, you will probably do the activities in class or for homework and then your teacher will correct them or go through them with you in class.

You can use the *Exam Maximiser* to check that you have learnt the grammar and vocabulary in each unit of the Coursebook, or to revise for tests and exams. The skills you'll work on in the Reading, Writing, Listening and Speaking sections will help you improve your language skills in general, and prepare for the exam.

CONTENTS

Unit	Grammar	Vocabulary	Reading
1 **Social networks** p.6	Present simple and present continuous p.7 State verbs p.7 Verb patterns: -ing and infinitive p.10	Collocations: communication; family relationships p.6	Multiple choice p.8
2 **Transformations** p.12	Present perfect and past simple p.14 Past simple, used to and would p.16	Describing feelings p.12 Dependent prepositions p.14	Gapped text p.14
3 **Passions** p.18	Countable/uncountable nouns; expressions of quantity p.19 Present perfect simple or continuous p.22	Collocations: pastimes p.18–19	Multiple matching p.21
4 **A sense of adventure** p.24	Narrative tenses: past simple, past continuous, past perfect p.26 Time phrases p.26 Subject/Object questions p.28	Extreme adjectives p.28	Multiple choice p.24
5 **The consumer society** p.30	Future forms: p.31 be used to/got used to p.34	Shops and shopping p.30	Gapped text p.33
6 **Working lives** p.36	Making comparisons p.39 Modals of obligation and necessity p.40	Finding a job p.36	Multiple matching p.38
7 **Well-being** p.42	Zero, first and second conditionals p.44 unless, otherwise, provided that p.45	Health and fitness p.43	Multiple choice p.46
8 **Nature study** p.48	Passive forms p.49 Causative have p.52	Animals p.48	Gapped text p.51
9 **Future society** p.54	Future perfect and continuous p.55 Reported speech p.58	Computers p.54	Multiple choice p.56
10 **Global culture** p.60	Relative pronouns and relative clauses p.62 Articles p.64	Arts and culture p.63	Multiple matching p.60
11 **Style and design** p.66	Modals of possibility and certainty p.67 so/such/very; too and enough p.70	Fashion and design p.66 Adjective order p.67	Gapped text p.68
12 **Science and discovery** p.72	Third conditional and wish p.74 Reporting verbs p.76	Research and discovery; science and scientists p.75–76	Multiple matching p.72

Social networks

Listening

Multiple choice ▶ CB page 7

1 ▶ **01 You will hear four people talking about some communication problems. For questions 1–4, choose the best answer, A, B or C.**

1 Why did the girl lose her job?
- **A** She spent too much time online.
- **B** She was not honest.
- **C** She had an illness.

2 Why was the girl upset?
- **A** She lost her mobile phone.
- **B** Her boyfriend was angry with her on the phone.
- **C** Strangers listened to a private phone call.

3 How did the boy feel about sending the postcard?
- **A** Surprised that it took so long to arrive.
- **B** Annoyed because he doesn't enjoy writing.
- **C** Embarrassed because it never reached his friend.

4 What did the girl do wrong?
- **A** She accidentally deleted a whole email.
- **B** She sent an email to the wrong people.
- **C** She wrote some angry things to her friend.

Vocabulary

collocations: communication; family members ▶ CB page 7

1 **Choose the correct alternative to complete the sentences.**

1 You must *start/get* in touch when you come to my city.

2 I've communicated with my French friend by email a lot but we've never met face *by/to* face.

3 My friend and I often go online to *chat/discuss* about nothing in particular.

4 If you *make/send* an email, make sure you've got the right address!

5 I've made some good friends at uni and I hope we don't *forget/lose* touch.

6 You must *download/record* Adele's new album – it's amazing!

7 When I have a day off, I like to visit Mum to *make/catch* up with news.

8 I like to *keep/bring* up-to-date with the latest fashion trends.

Grammar
present simple and present continuous ▶ CB page 8

1 **Choose the correct options to complete sentences 1–8.**

1 I *am not going/don't go* to the school reunion next month.

2 Shh! I *speak/'m speaking* to your aunt on the phone.

3 Tara *has/is having* a hard time trying to get the phone company to replace her mobile.

4 I *find/am finding* it easy to misunderstand what people mean in text messages.

5 Miguel *is being/is* a real whizz on the computer – he can do anything!

6 Jenny's flight *leaves/is leaving* at three o'clock. She's going to visit her cousin in Australia.

7 It *is becoming/becomes* harder and harder to keep in touch with old friends.

8 I *visit/'m visiting* my cousin in hospital tonight.

2 **Read the email below about a school reunion. Complete the text with the present simple or present continuous form of the verb in brackets.**

Hi, Suzana!

I **(1)** .... (*look forward to*) the school reunion next week! **(2)** .... you .... (*come*)? I hope so! I'm so happy that our old school **(3)** .... (*organise*) such an exciting event. I **(4)** .... (*remember*) so much about our school days! I **(5)** .... (*be*) out of touch with some of our old friends now, so I can't wait to talk to everyone face to face about what they **(6)** .... (*do*) these days.

The party **(7)** .... (*start*) at seven o'clock, so if you like, I can pick you up after I **(8)** .... (*finish*) work at six. Let me know!

Love,

Zena

3 **Look at the verbs in brackets in Activity 2. Do they describe states (S) or actions (A)?**

4 **Circle the state verbs in the box.**

chat   communicate   depend   do   hear
like   lose   own   phone   smell

Use of English
Multiple-choice cloze ▶ CB page 9

About the exam:
In the exam, you have to read a text with eight gaps and choose from four possible answers to fill each gap.

Strategy:
• Read the title and the text first for meaning.
• Think about what kind of word might fit in each gap (e.g. a noun, a verb, an adjective, a conjunction, etc.).
• Look at the words immediately before and after each gap to help you.
• Think about words that often go together (collocations), for example: *to catch a bus*.

1 **Read the text and decide which answer (A, B, C or D) fits each gap.**

BLOG ▶

I LOVE MY MOBILE PHONE

I just love my mobile phone and I **(0)** *spend* hours every day texting friends and chatting on the internet. My parents think I waste too much time playing around on my phone **(1)** .... I should be doing more **(2)** .... things like schoolwork! But I **(3)** .... online to look things up and it's really helpful talking to my friends about what we're doing at school. My parents don't agree **(4)** .... me, though! My favourite app is the music app. I've got all my music **(5)** .... on my phone so I can listen to my favourite tracks **(6)** .... when I'm in bed before I go to sleep. It helps me relax. I also love taking photos on my phone, which I share with all my friends on Facebook. I've got loads now – I just can't seem to have **(7)** .... It's like my own personal photo **(8)** .... of my life!

0	**A** spend	**B** use	**C** have	**D** do
1	**A** although	**B** while	**C** during	**D** despite
2	**A** important	**B** busy	**C** good	**D** popular
3	**A** wait	**B** arrive	**C** visit	**D** go
4	**A** on	**B** for	**C** with	**D** at
5	**A** collected	**B** carried	**C** supplied	**D** stored
6	**A** quietly	**B** finally	**C** immediately	**D** slowly
7	**A** enough	**B** plenty	**C** several	**D** some
8	**A** experience	**B** diary	**C** time	**D** adventure

Reading
Multiple choice ▶ CB pages 10–11

1 **Look at the picture. What is a holiday rep?**

2 **Read the title of the article. What kind of information do you think will be included?**

3 **Read the whole article quickly and answer the questions.**

1 What sort of people is the job of holiday rep **not** suitable for?

....

2 How old do you need to be to have a job like this?

....

3 Apart from English, which other languages are mentioned in the article?

....

4 Where can you find advertisements for jobs as a holiday rep?

....

5 What do holiday companies give their reps free?

....

6 What hotel facilities are mentioned in the article?

....

4 **Read the whole article. For questions 1–6, choose the answer (A or B) which you think fits best according to the text.**

1 According to Angela, what is the most important quality for a holiday rep?
- **A** having a confident personality
- **B** enjoying responsibility

2 Angela uses the examples of France and South America to show us that holiday reps
- **A** have to be flexible.
- **B** have to work long hours.

3 Angela was surprised to get her job as a holiday rep because she
- **A** only had a basic travel qualification.
- **B** could only speak one language.

4 In the second paragraph, Angela says that she
- **A** hadn't travelled a lot in her free time.
- **B** didn't know much about other countries.

5 Angela says that in an interview you should
- **A** make yourself sound better than you are.
- **B** be honest about what you know.

6 What does Angela like most about being a holiday rep?
- **A** meeting people from different places
- **B** getting free access to facilities

5 **Look at the phrasal verbs underlined in the article and decide which meaning (A or B) is closest to the meaning in the article.**

1 believe in
- **A** be certain that something exists
- **B** be certain about an ability

2 deal with
- **A** solve a problem
- **B** be concerned about

3 send out
- **A** put in the post
- **B** advertise

4 stand out
- **A** be easy to see
- **B** be better than others

5 find out
- **A** discover
- **B** recover

6 get on with
- **A** continue doing
- **B** have a good relationship

So you want to be a holiday rep? Read on …

My name's Angela and I'm a holiday rep. I love my job and it's the best way to make friends with people from all over the world. Holiday reps are responsible for making sure that the customer has a fantastic holiday. As a rep, you represent the holiday company you're working for, so above everything else, you have to be friendly, sociable and believe in yourself. You also have to be able to deal with all kinds of situations and if you're impatient or like regular working hours then this isn't the job for you! In addition, you have to be ready to go anywhere in the world – you don't get to choose where you work. For example, one month you might be in the south of France and the next in South America!

You need to be at least eighteen to become a rep and although formal qualifications aren't necessary, getting a basic certificate in travel and tourism (like I did) will always be useful because there's a lot of competition for jobs. It's not as easy as you might think to get a job in the travel industry. It's helpful if you can speak other languages, especially French or Spanish. I only speak English, so I didn't really expect to get a job – but I did! It helps if you travel a lot yourself too. I didn't have much chance to do that before I became a rep, though I do have a good knowledge of where places are in the world.

There are a few ways you can find work as a holiday rep. Newspapers and travel magazines often advertise positions. And don't forget the internet, which is probably the most useful source of information! Travel companies send out application forms to people who are interested in working for them – read the form carefully and make sure your application stands out. If you do get an interview, remember, you must answer questions truthfully – you'll quickly get found out if you pretend you can speak Greek or are familiar with a country you've never even heard of! One thing you should avoid is saying you want the job to get free holidays! It sounds silly but you'd be surprised by how many people actually say that.

There are lots of cool things about being a holiday rep. The pay isn't the best in the world but in my opinion the benefits of the job are worth far more than the pay packet. You get to see some amazing places and the people are fantastic – I keep in touch with a lot of the customers I look after. The nightlife with the other reps and customers can be fun too, if you get on with them! You get free accommodation as a rep. Don't be too excited about this – I'm staying in a tent in my current job, which isn't the most comfortable place to stay! You also get a uniform but the greatest thing of all for me is that you get to use the facilities in the resort you're working at – brilliant if there's a swimming pool or tennis courts because you don't have to pay to use them.

Grammar
verb patterns ▶ CB page 12

1 **Complete the postcard with the correct form of the words in the box. Use -ing or the infinitive with or without to.**

| do | eat | fish | go | see (x2) | spend | swim |

Hi, Andrei!
I'm here on holiday in Hungary with my family – my grandparents are Hungarian, so it's great to be with people who know the country really well. We're staying in a cottage in the countryside and there's a lake nearby where we enjoy **(1)** .... every morning. I'd love **(2)** .... this at home too, but there's nowhere fun to go.
   I'm also learning **(3)** ....! I'm not usually keen on fishing but my granddad makes it great fun. **(4)** .... all day in the sun is pretty tiring, so before we have dinner we take a short nap. I like **(5)** .... outdoors – the food definitely tastes better!
   I'm looking forward to **(6)** .... you. Let's **(7)** .... that new action film when I get back. I'd better **(8)** .... now.
See you soon!
Pete

2 **Find and correct the mistakes with infinitives in the sentences. There is one mistake in each sentence.**

1 We'd better not to be late home from school – we're visiting Grandma this evening.

2 I'd love go to Kenya on holiday. I've never been to Africa.

3 I can't wait get my new phone – it's got some fantastic apps!

4 Let's to buy a present for Dad's birthday. What do you think he would like?

5 Stephanie's hoping pass her Travel and Tourism exam. She worked really hard.

6 Jo's learning be a tour guide. He wants to work in Spain.

7 I've arranged have a new website built for my work.

8 You should to check your passport is valid before you travel.

Speaking
Interview: Giving personal information
▶ CB page 13

About the exam:
In the exam, the examiner asks you some general questions about yourself: where you live and your hobbies, plans or experiences.

Strategy:
• Try to give an answer that is not too short but also that is not long and complicated.
• Try to make a good impression and avoid making basic grammar mistakes.
• Do not learn and practise a speech about yourself. It is better to listen and answer the questions directly.

1 **Match questions 1–10 with answers A–H. There are two questions with no answers.**

1 Where are you from? ....

2 What do you like about living there? ....

3 Do you watch much television? Why/Why not? ....

4 How do you like to keep fit? ....

5 What did you do on your last birthday? ....

6 What is your main ambition? ....

7 Are you very interested in fashion? ....

8 Tell us something about your best friend. ....

9 Where do you like to spend your holidays? Why? ....

10 Do you have a favourite hobby? What is it? ....

A It's very peaceful and the people are very friendly. Everyone knows each other. It's really pretty too.

B France. My home is in Beaulieu, a small village just outside Bordeaux. It's close to a lovely forest.

C I think I'd like to be a teacher of primary school children. I'd like to teach them English.

D Not a lot. I prefer to spend my time with my friends, playing games and chatting.

E I prefer to go somewhere nice and hot where I can relax. Like Spain or Italy.

F I do a lot of painting and drawing – especially cartoons. I draw cartoons of famous people and give them to my friends. It's fun!

G I'm not very worried about what I wear. I like trendy things but I don't spend a lot of time thinking about clothes.

H I went to a big hotel with my family and we had a lovely meal there. It was good.

Writing
Essay (Part 1) ▶ CB page 14

About the exam:
In the exam, you have to write an essay in Part 1. There will be a question for you to answer and then two points that you must include in your essay. You also need to add one more point of your own.

Strategy:
Make sure you use all the notes in your essay. You must also give reasons for your opinions.

1 **Read the exam task and use the words in the box to complete the essay.**

> In your English class, you have been talking about what makes a good friend. Now your English teacher has asked you to write an essay. Write an essay using all the notes and give reasons for your point of view.
>
> **Essay question:**
> *Are old friends always the best friends?*
>
> **Notes:**
>
> Things to write about:
>
> 1 shared experiences
> 2 different personalities
> 3 your own idea

Because   For   However   matter   mean
reason   so   think   true

As we get older, we go to different schools, begin new jobs and even start families. We meet a lot of different people and make new friends all the time, (1) .... usually our social network includes people we have met at many different times in our lives. But are the oldest friends really the best?

For some people, I (2) .... this is true. The (3) .... I say this is because these friends know you better than anyone else. They have shared important experiences with you and sometimes they know you better than you know yourself! (4) .... of that, they can give really good advice.

(5) ...., this is not always the case. Someone may have known you very well in the past but that does not (6) .... that they know you very well now. Perhaps you have both changed. This is especially (7) .... if you have been out of touch for a while. (8) .... me, the best friends are the ones you can rely on to give you support and to tell you the truth. It doesn't (9) .... whether you've known them for ten months or ten years.

2 **Underline phrases in the essay that show the writer has done everything the exam task asks.**

3 **Match the following phrases with their functions.**

1 Many people feel that …   ....
2 That is why …   ....
3 I strongly believe that …   ....
4 Alternatively, …   ....
5 In addition to this, …   ....
6 For instance, …   ....

A introducing a contrasting opinion or example
B giving an example
C adding to something you've said
D giving a general point of view
E giving a reason
F giving your opinion

4 **Read the exam task and think of a point of your own to include. Then make notes and write your essay. Write 140–190 words.**

> In your English class, you have been talking about who it is best to ask for advice. Now your teacher has asked you to write an essay. Write an essay using all the notes and give reasons for your point of view.
>
> **Essay question:**
> *Is it better to ask family or friends for advice?*
>
> **Notes:**
>
> Things to write about:
>
> 1 type of problem
> 2 relationships
> 3 your own idea

Transformations

Vocabulary

describing feelings ▶ CB page 16

1 **Choose the correct option to complete the sentences.**

1 I was *surprised/surprising* when Eddy gave me a present because he never usually remembers my birthday!

2 We were *confused/confusing* by the instructions in the test and we didn't know what to do.

3 I lent my umbrella to Eva and she lost it. I was very *annoyed/annoying*.

4 We worked until midnight on the project. It was *exhausting/exhausted*.

5 At the fancy dress party, Fred wore a tiger suit. It was very *amusing/amused*.

6 Someone spilt coffee all over Greta's new dress. She was very *upsetting/upset*.

2 **Complete the sentences with the correct form of the words in brackets.**

1 I love the history of fashion! I think it's .... (*fascinate*) to see how clothes have changed over the years.

2 Jenny always gets .... (*worry*) before acting in a play. She thinks she'll forget her lines.

3 If someone says I look good or they like my new outfit, I get .... (*embarrass*) and go red!

4 I can't watch horror films because I get .... (*scare*) when I go to bed!

5 Pete was in a TV competition and he was .... (*thrill*) when he won £1,000.

6 When I saw my bad test results I got a bit .... (*depress*) but I'm OK now.

3 **Which two adjectives from Activity 2 are positive?**

Speaking

Long turn ▶ CB page 17

About the exam:

In the exam, you have to talk on your own for about a minute. You have to compare two pictures and answer a question.

Strategy:

• Don't describe the pictures in detail but compare them and then answer the question.

• You can easily remind yourself of the question because it is printed above your pictures.

1 ▶ 02 **Listen to the instruction an examiner gives to a candidate and complete what he says.**

Your pictures show people who have **(1)** .... for different reasons.

Compare the pictures and say why the people **(2)** .... to change their appearance.

2 ▶ 03 **Choose the correct options to complete the candidate's answer. Then listen and check.**

(1) *Both/Two* pictures show people who look different from the way they normally look, but **(2)** *on/in* the first picture, the little girl is still changing her appearance **(3)** *whereas/although* in the second picture the people have completely changed already. The little girl is probably getting ready for a party or for a celebration with her friends. I think it **(4)** *perhaps/might* be Hallowe'en or something like that. **(5)** *So/Because*, she wants to look different for fun. An older person, it might be her mum, is putting some bright make-up on her face. I think the little girl looks **(6)** *excited/exciting*! She's probably been looking forward to this for a long time. And little girls always love to dress up! The people in the other picture, **(7)** *however/but*, need to look different because it's their job. They are actors in a play. I think it's a funny play and maybe there's some singing and dancing in it too. They **(8)** *look/look like* very happy. Perhaps the audience is clapping. I don't think they needed to change their appearance much – just put on some clothes from a different time and change their hairstyles.

Listening
Sentence completion ▶ CB page 18

1 **Look at part of an exam task and answer the questions.**

> You will hear part of an interview with a woman called Suzy who is talking about winning the lottery.

1 How many speakers will you hear? ....

2 Which person will give you the answers to the questions? ....

3 What did this person do? ....

2 **Look at 1–6 in the text. What kind of word do you think might go in each gap?**

LOTTERY WINNER

Suzy bought her first lottery ticket at the local **(1)** .... Suzy felt **(2)** .... because she wasn't sure how to spend her money. The first thing Suzy bought for herself was a **(3)** .... Paying for a new **(4)** .... pleased Suzy the most. Buying a **(5)** .... helped a member of Suzy's family in their work.

Suzy's first trip to a foreign country was to **(6)** ....

3 ▶ 04 **Listen to the recording and complete the sentences. Then check your answers to Activity 2.**

Vocabulary

dependent prepositions ▶ CB page 18

1 **Choose the correct option (A, B or C) to complete the sentences.**

1 Which company do you work _____?
   A of   B by   C for

2 Don't make jokes _____ Paul's new hairstyle!
   A about   B across   C on

3 Can you think _____ a word that ends in -ism?
   A up   B at   C of

4 Tom ran _____ from the police after he stole the money.
   A along   B away   C after

5 The children laughed _____ the dog in the funny hat!
   A over   B at   C up

6 I agree _____ Sally about the right answer.
   A about   B with   C on

7 I don't care _____ about the money, I just want an interesting job.
   A of   B over   C about

8 We arrived _____ the hotel just before lunchtime.
   A to   B in   C at

Grammar

present perfect and past simple
▶ CB page 19

1 **Match sentences and questions 1–6 with replies A–F.**

1 Have you ever bought a lottery ticket? _____

2 Gareth's got a new job working for an advertising company. _____

3 Have you thought about who you'll invite to your party yet? _____

4 I've never been to a tennis match, have you? _____

5 I've been scared of cats since one scratched me.

6 Sheila's been to South America, you know. _____

A No, I haven't. Have you?

B I went to one two weeks ago, actually.

C Yes, she said she loved it!

D Yes, I wrote the invitations last night.

E I've never liked them myself.

F I know, he told me last week.

2 **Correct the mistakes with the present perfect and past simple in the sentences. There is one mistake in each sentence.**

1 I've been to London on a business trip last week.

2 Life changed over the last few years for animals that live in the Polar Regions.

3 I did wear cool clothes when I was a teenager.

4 Megan has got up early this morning and did her homework before lunch.

5 The town I live in grew a lot since I've lived here.

6 People became more and more conscious of the need for responsible tourism.

7 Gina has bought some new glasses at the weekend. They look great!

8 The invention of the wheel has changed the world forever.

Reading

Gapped text ▶ CB pages 20–21

About the exam:
In the exam, you will read a text with six missing sentences. You need to choose the correct sentences from a list to fill the gaps. There will be one extra sentence which you do not need to use.

Strategy:
Look carefully at the sentences before and after the gaps and use words such as *it/he/they/this*, etc. to help you choose.

1 **Read the article about tourism in Antarctica quickly and choose the best answer (A, B or C).**

Why are more people visiting the Antarctic these days?

A New technology lets us go there all through the year.

B Travel articles show us how beautiful the place is.

C People want to see it before environmental changes affect it.

2 **Read the first paragraph of the article again. What do the words in bold refer to?**

1 **one** refers to _____

2 **This** refers to _____

3 **it** refers to _____

4 **them** refers to _____

3 **Read the article again. Choose from sentences A–F the one which fits each gap 1–5. There is one extra sentence which you do not need to use.**

TO COLDLY GO

Tourism is <u>damaging</u> Antarctica. We should protect this unspoilt place by limiting the numbers of people allowed to visit.

There has been a rush of 'see it before it's gone' tourism in recent years. The popularity of 'climate tourism' has certainly been encouraged by travel journalism. In March, one newspaper had a travel article with the headline: *Global warming: 10 places to see before it's too late.* Last year, another newspaper had **one** called *10 wonders of the disappearing world.* **This** described <u>threatened</u> places such as Mount Kilimanjaro and the Maldives – and then **it** told you how to get to **them**!

This is a worrying, although understandable, trend. I too would love to see some of these places with my own eyes. Who wouldn't? On the top of my list would be Antarctica. I grew up amazed by the adventures of Amundsen, Shackleton, and Scott. [1] When people learn that these places may be changed by the climate in the near future, they suddenly want to visit them. I can easily understand the reason behind this type of tourism – just as I can understand why people want to climb to the top of mountains or reach out into space. But if tourists are making a bad situation worse, then they shouldn't be allowed to go.

Antarctica is one place where I believe that this is true more than anywhere else. [2] It is too environmentally <u>fragile</u> for the heavy feet of tourists! It is also one of the only places in the world that hasn't got a human population – so it doesn't need tourism for the money.

The sea ice is disappearing and it will soon be possible to reach more places by sea. [3] This will allow tourist activities to grow. Over 80 percent of tourists actually land on Antarctica during their voyages and therefore the risk to the fragile environment is increasing.

For decades, the country received just a few tourists. However, in recent years, it has become extremely popular as a <u>destination</u> for cruise ships, encouraged by the continual demand for 'adventure tourism'. Last year more than 35,000 tourists stepped ashore from their cruise ships in Antarctica.

One visitor wrote recently, with childish <u>glee</u>, about how he is now the proud owner of a small stone that he picked up when visiting Antarctica. He had strong opinions about tourism here.

[4] I strongly disagree: I believe in being careful. We must show that we can be responsible tourists in other places first before we spoil this beautiful place.

Surely, we don't always need to 'have' something just because we know it's there and as a result, end up damaging it. (And no, I don't agree with the view that you have to see these things with your own eyes to really understand why they need protecting. [5]) I fear, though, that this is an unrealistic hope. Companies are buying bigger and stronger ships to carry their tourists to Antarctica. The force of tourism is perhaps more <u>powerful</u> than that of a glacier.

A He argued that the continent shouldn't only be open to scientists.

B This means that the tourist season will get longer.

C It would surely be a wonderful personal experience to follow in their footsteps.

D Although these rules are good, it is unlikely that anyone will obey them.

E I've never seen the Brazilian rainforest, but I understand why it shouldn't be cut down.

F In fact, I believe it is the one place in the world where there should now be a strict 'no tourism' rule.

4 Match the underlined words in the article with definitions 1–6.

1 joy, happiness, delight ....
2 a place tourists go to ....
3 weak, easily broken ....
4 in danger ....
5 hurting ....
6 strong ....

Grammar
past simple, *used to* and *would*
▶ CB page 22

1 **Choose the correct option to complete the sentences.**

1 When I was a child I *used to/would* have blond hair but now it's dark brown.

2 Tommy *went/used to go* to Rome last week on holiday. Lucky him!

3 I *used to/would* love sitting by the fire listening to my grandma telling stories.

4 Michaela *said/used to say* she enjoyed the party on Saturday.

5 Tina *sent/would send* Angelo a text to arrange a time to meet last night.

6 On Saturday, Grace and Joe *had/would have* a meal in a restaurant and then saw a film.

2 **Complete the text with the correct form of *used to* or *would*. Sometimes both are possible.**

LOG ▶ What did you **(1)** .... want to be when you were a kid? I wanted to be a professional footballer. Even when I was really little, I **(2)** .... spend hours kicking a ball around in the street where I lived. I **(3)** .... have the best football or the smartest trainers but I had so much energy and passion for the sport. My mum **(4)** .... have to come and find me at mealtimes – I didn't hear her calling because I was so absorbed in my practice! I **(5)** .... watch every match on TV and I **(6)** .... know the names of all the footballers. Sometimes my dad **(7)** .... take me to watch a live match and I loved it! I **(8)** .... have a really powerful kick but then I got injured and that was the end of my dreams of becoming a professional player. I still watch my team but I don't play anymore. I'm more into music these days and now I want to be a rock star!

Use of English
Open cloze ▶ CB page 23

About the exam:
In the exam, you have to read a text and fill in eight missing words.

Strategy:
· Remember that the title gives you clues about the topic of the text.
· Before you start reading, think about what ideas might be mentioned in the text.
· Read the whole text first for meaning and think about which word might go in each gap.
· Remember that the missing words may be parts of verbs (e.g. give *up*), linking words (e.g. *and*, *but*) or vocabulary such as a collocation (e.g. *do a project*).

1 **Look at the title of the article in Activity 3. What is the article about?**

2 **Look at the words in the box and decide if they are linking words, verbs, pronouns, prepositions or articles.**

| are | have | make | out | than | the | them | While |

3 **Complete the text with words from the box in Activity 2.**

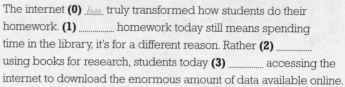
How the internet has transformed
homework

The internet **(0)** *has* truly transformed how students do their homework. **(1)** .... homework today still means spending time in the library, it's for a different reason. Rather **(2)** .... using books for research, students today **(3)** .... accessing the internet to download the enormous amount of data available online.

In the past, students were limited to their school's selection of books and it could be very annoying to get to the library only to find out that someone had already taken the book you needed. The internet, though, never runs **(4)** .... of information. However, students do have to **(5)** .... sure that the information they find online is true. Teachers **(6)** .... also benefited from homework being done on the internet. Instead of carrying students' work around with **(7)** ...., online systems allow students to electronically upload their work for teachers to read. Of course, this also means that students can no longer use **(8)** .... excuse that the dog ate their homework!

Writing

Informal letter ▶ CB page 24

About the exam:
In Part 2 of the exam, you must choose one of three questions to answer. One question may be to write a letter or email in response to part of a letter or email you have received. This may be informal or semi-formal.

Strategy:
Make sure you deal with all the points that are made in the email or letter extract.

1 **Read the exam task and the answer. Choose the correct options to complete the letter.**

> You have received a letter from your Scottish friend, Gemma. Read this part of the letter and then write your letter to Gemma.
> Write **140–190** words.

> We've just moved into our new house and there's lots of work to do. At least we can choose how it looks, though. What would you do to make your dream house?
>
> Love,
>
> Billy

Hi, Billy,

I thought I'd drop you a line to **(1)** *make/let* you know what I'd do in my perfect new house! You know that I love nature, so **(2)** *as/like* you can imagine, for me, the most important thing is the front garden. I'd like the first thing I see to be grass and flowers and things. When we moved here, I asked Tom and Fran to come round and we did the work on the garden together. It **(3)** *went/happened* really well.

The next thing I'd do would be paint all the rooms bright colours. I'd use a different colour for every room. In fact, you'll never **(4)** *think/guess* what colour I've just painted my bedroom here. Bright purple! Apart from that, there would be candles everywhere. I **(5)** *very/absolutely* love them. I think they add warmth to a room.

Anyway, how's your decorating going? Something **(6)** *says/tells* me that you're going to be busy for months! Do write soon with your **(7)** *news/information*. I can come and stay and help you out with any work you've got to do if you like!

(8) *A lot/Lots* of love,

Gemma

2 **Which of the phrases 1–8 would you NOT find in an informal letter?**

1 I was delighted to receive your letter.
2 Thanks for your lovely, long letter.
3 I must also tell you about …
4 Would you kindly send me …
5 We had a really good time.
6 I look forward to your reply.
7 See you soon, …
8 Yours sincerely, …

3 **Read the exam task and write the letter in 140–190 words.**

> You have received this letter from your English friend, Max. Read this part of the letter and then write your letter to Max.
> Write **140–190** words.

> I've decided to completely change my bedroom! I want a new colour scheme and a new style of furniture. Mum and Dad are paying for it and say I can do anything I like! You're really creative — any suggestions?
>
> Love,
>
> Max

Passions

Listening

Multiple matching ▶ CB page 27

1 ▶ 05 **You are going to hear four people speaking about cookery classes they run at a college. Listen and match headings A–D with speakers 1–4.**

A   Only the best!   Speaker 1 ☐
B   Eat well, stay well!   Speaker 2 ☐
C   Fattening but fun!   Speaker 3 ☐
D   Eat for less!   Speaker 4 ☐

2 ▶ 05 **Listen again and choose from the list A–E what each speaker 1–4 says. There is one extra letter which you do not need to use.**

A   I hope to change people's lifestyles.
B   My students are not satisfied with easy recipes.
C   I cannot teach all the students who want to   Speaker 1 ☐
     attend my class.   Speaker 2 ☐
D   My first teacher was a chef on a TV cookery   Speaker 3 ☐
     programme.   Speaker 4 ☐
E   I teach an unlikely combination of students.

Vocabulary

collocations ▶ CB page 27

1 **Complete the second sentences with the word given so that they have a similar meaning to the first.**

1   In the beginning it was difficult to hit the ball in a straight line, but I got better!
    TOUGH
    It .... first to hit the ball in a straight line, but I got better.

2   Acting is my real love!
    PASSIONATE
    I'm .... acting!

3   I nearly gave up learning German at school because it was hard. However, I didn't and now I speak it well!
    STUCK
    I nearly gave up learning German when I was at school because it was hard. However, ... and now I speak it well.

4   You can't become a top chef in only a few years.
    LIFETIME
    It .... to become a top chef.

5   I became addicted to computer games when I was ten.
    HOOKED
    I .... when I was ten.

2 Complete sentences 1–8 with the correct form of *do*, *go* or *play*.

1 Some of my friends .... voluntary work at the weekends.

2 My parents never .... clubbing when they were my age!

3 Do you fancy .... cards this evening? I'm not going out.

4 I can't .... this crossword. It's way too difficult.

5 My brother .... cricket every Saturday afternoon.

6 I'd like to .... an evening class in car maintenance.

7 We're .... skiing next month in France. I hope the snow's good.

8 My friend's sister is .... karate at school. She's really good.

3 Complete the text with the correct prepositions.

CUP STACKING CHAMPIONSHIPS

If you're interested **(1)** .... seeing young people who are passionate **(2)** .... their hobby and who are also amazingly good **(3)** .... it, then don't miss the finals of the National Cup Stacking competition at Swindon Arts centre this Saturday afternoon. This is fast becoming a really popular activity and kids everywhere are mad **(4)** .... it. This Saturday, contestants from all over the country will show us their skill by putting cups on top of each other as quickly as they possibly can when they compete **(5)** .... the nationals. You'll be fascinated **(6)** .... their speed! Think you'd be hopeless **(7)** .... it? Try it yourself after the competition when some of the youngsters will hold a teaching session aimed at getting us all **(8)** .... cup stacking!

Grammar
countable and uncountable nouns
▶ CB page 28

1 Read the article and look at the underlined nouns. Are they countable (C) or uncountable (U)?

▶ BLOG ▶

I'm really lucky to work in a job I love. I teach at a college which offers a fantastic range of evening classes for adults. I've always been passionate about **(1)** languages, especially my own – English. At the moment I'm working with a group of adults who, for various reasons, missed out on schooling when they were younger and fell behind in their reading and writing **(2)** skills. I don't earn much **(3)** money but what I love about teaching this class is the students' desire to catch up. Also, they're really creative in their **(4)** work because they have life **(5)** experience. They're an interesting group of **(6)** people – they soak up **(7)** knowledge and are keen to get the qualifications they didn't get when they were younger. It's really inspiring and quite different from teaching **(8)** children.

2 Look at the words in the box. Which of them are abstract (ideas or thoughts) and which of them are concrete (objects you can touch)?

bread   love   news   oil   pasta   silver
skills   values

3 Complete the sentences with the words from the box in Activity 2.

1 Caroline has learned a great new recipe for .... and sauce in her Italian cooking class.

2 I've learned how to top up my car with .... in the car maintenance workshop.

3 Steve listens to the .... every day – he likes to know what's happening in the world.

4 I've baked .... to eat with the soup. I hope you like it!

5 Zeke's into making jewellery from .... for men.

6 Doing an evening class is a great way to develop new ....

7 Your .... are the things you believe in.

8 Dina and Ned share a .... of playing sport.

expressions of quantity ▶ CB page 28

4 **Complete the sentences with *a/an, some, any, much, many, few/a few, a lot of/lots of* and *little/a little*. Sometimes there may be more than one correct answer.**

1 There's .... fashion design course you might be interested in at my college. I'll give you .... information about it next time I see you.

2 Chris, can you add milk to the shopping list? There isn't .... left. We need .... biscuits too. Oh, and can you get .... oranges?

3 There's only .... coffee in the jar – would you like tea instead?

4 Jen, do you have .... guitar music I could borrow? I really want to learn to play.

5 .... children seem to enjoy playing outside these days. It's a pity.

6 How .... people were at the pool today? There weren't .... when I went the other day.

5 **Find and correct the mistakes in sentences 1–6. There is one mistake in each sentence.**

1 I don't have many interest in sport, I'm afraid.

2 How much times have you run a marathon?

3 There are lots of cheese in the fridge if you fancy a snack.

4 Do you have albums by Justin Bieber? He's so cool.

5 I love listening to little classical music to relax.

6 I've got lot of hobbies and I'm always busy at the weekends.

Speaking
Collaborative task ▶ CB page 29

1 **Read the exam task and say if comments 1–6 are *true* (T) or *false* (F).**

> Here are some different types of competition. First, talk about what preparation people need to do before these different types of competition. Then decide which types of competition make people feel most nervous.

1 You have to talk about what the people have done before the competitions. ....

2 You have to say whether you would like to do these competitions. ....

3 You have to take turns to give your own opinions. ....

4 You have to talk about how the people feel when they do these competitions. ....

5 You have to make a decision together. ....

2 **Match the students' comments 1–5 with the types of competition they're talking about A–E.**

A sport
D talent show
B in class
C board games
E playground games

1 I think you need to train really hard before you do this kind of competiton because you need to be very fit. ....

2 Some people don't need any training because they have natural talent, but others need classes, I imagine. ....

3 These are just friendly games so I don't think people have prepared very much at all for them. ....

4 Sometimes people just play at home for fun but sometimes they can have serious competitions. Then they have to practise a lot. ....

5 It depends. If it's just a quick class test then they don't have to prepare a lot but if it's a big exam then yes, they have to do lots of revision. ....

3 **Complete the useful phrases with the correct words from the box.**

about	agree	choose	for	in	let's
on	point	think	what		

1 .... begin with …
2 What .... this one?
3 .... my opinion …
4 Do you .... ?
5 Let's move ....
6 Don't you .... ?
7 That's a good ....
8 .... do you think …
9 .... me, it's the TV show.
10 So, that's the one we .... ?

4 **Match the phrases in Activity 3 to headings A–C.**

A Organising the discussion ....
B Involving your partner ....
C Giving an opinion ....

Reading

Multiple matching ▶ CB pages 30–31

1 Read the magazine article about famous people who have done difficult things to raise money for charity. Which celebrity (A, B or C) raised the least money?

Every year celebrities push themselves to the limit – all because of a passion to help charities. Here are three of them.

A Eddie Izzard

Eddie Izzard is better known for his comedy and acting skills than his running! However, Eddie decided to set himself a big challenge to try to raise a lot of money for charity. He <u>set out</u> to run 43 marathons across the UK. His aim was to run one marathon every day, six days a week and he nearly did it! In fact it took him slightly longer – 51 days. A challenge like this would be difficult for an experienced runner and Eddie had very little experience! When he decided to <u>go ahead</u> with the marathons he was rather overweight and hadn't done much running before. Some fitness experts worked out a nine month programme for him to prepare but Eddie only had five weeks! So, he trained hard and then set out on the challenge of a lifetime. And he succeeded. Despite blisters and sore toes he ran and ran and returned home triumphant. He believes that it was his determination not to <u>give up</u> that saw him through the challenge – as well as the fear of <u>letting</u> <u>down</u> his charity. He <u>ended up</u> raising more than £200,000 online. Well done, Eddie!

B Matt Baker

Imagine cycling 16 hours a day for eight days from Edinburgh in Scotland to London. Then imagine that you are pulling a rickshaw behind you and most of the time there is a passenger in it! This was the task that Matt Baker, a TV presenter, set himself last year to raise money for charity. Luckily, Matt was quite fit to start with. However, after the exhausting ride he had lost weight, was suffering from lack of sleep and had a very sore bottom! Matt is certain that he could not have finished the task without the encouragement of people who lined the roads to watch him – even at night in the pouring rain. He was amazed by people's generosity. Many just pushed money into his hands and pockets as he rode past. Matt finished the challenge having raised over a million pounds. But he never wants to see a rickshaw again!

C David Walliams

David Walliams is a popular TV comedy actor who has spent a lot of time in recent years doing swimming challenges for charity. He has raised large amounts of money by swimming across the English Channel and the Straits of Gibraltar and in 2012 he swam 140 miles along the Thames River, finishing at Westminster Bridge in central London. David completed this marathon swim in eight days and it certainly wasn't an easy challenge. Because of the cold summer, the water temperature was low. When his skin started turning blue he had to wear a wetsuit! Then after a short time he <u>picked up</u> a stomach illness. The Thames isn't the cleanest river! In spite of a fever and sickness David continued. Luckily, he got better and completed his journey. Thousands and thousands of people cheered as he swam past and the final total donated to his online campaign raised was £1.1 million. What will it be next, David? Across the Atlantic?!

2 Read the article again and write A, B or C for questions 1–6.

Which celebrity

had <u>someone with him</u> for most of his challenge?	1
needed to <u>lose weight</u>?	2
was given some money <u>directly</u>?	3
has <u>experience</u> of doing sporting challenges for charity?	4
attracted <u>spectators</u> in spite of the <u>time and weather</u>?	5
recovered from a <u>health problem</u> during the challenge?	6

3 Complete sentences 1–6 with the correct form of the underlined phrasal verbs in the article. Use the word in brackets to help you.

1 When I was in Spain on holiday, I .... (*caught*) an illness and I was in bed for a week.

2 I think I really .... (*disappointed*) my mum and dad when I failed my exams last year.

3 We decided to .... (*continue*) with our plans to run ten miles for charity although the weather was terrible.

4 We got lost on our walk and .... (*found ourselves*) five kilometres away from home!

5 I .... (*planned*) to revise for three hours every day but I never did the full three!

6 I spent ages yesterday looking for our dog, which had run away. I nearly .... (*stopped*) but then I heard barking in the trees behind our house.

Grammar

present perfect simple or continuous
▶ CB page 32

1 Choose the correct option to complete the sentences.

1 I*'ve been counting/'ve counted* up the money we raised for charity. I'll carry on after lunch.

2 Have you ever *tried/been trying* gardening? It's not as boring as people think.

3 Sue *has trained/has been training* for the marathon for weeks.

4 I*'ve been ringing/'ve rung* Maria all afternoon. I think she's at the gym.

2 Complete the text with the past simple, present perfect simple or present perfect continuous form of the verb in brackets.

UNUSUAL HOBBIES: CLOG DANCING

I'm passionate about rhythm and I **(1)** .... (*always be*) into dance forms that are percussive – in other words, where you make a noise on the floor with your feet! I **(2)** .... (*do*) tap dance classes since I was ten and more recently I **(3)** .... (*take up*) clog dancing – a traditional form of dance that, where I come from, **(4)** .... (*grow up*) in factories in the late 1800s. The story goes that factory workers, who **(5)** .... (*wear*) wooden shoes for work, started dancing in them and imitated the sounds that the factory machines made.
In fact, clog dancing **(6)** .... (*probably be*) around for hundreds of years and over the last decade or so, it **(7)** .... (*make*) a comeback in the UK. There are festivals all over the country and my dance group **(8)** .... (*just raise*) over £1,000 for charity by doing a 'dance-a-thon', where we danced non-stop for twelve hours! Since then, we **(9)** .... (*work*) really hard on a new dance routine and we're going to enter a competition. We'll be on stage in front of hundreds of people – I **(10)** .... (*never feel*) so nervous! It'll be great fun, though.

Use of English
Word formation ▶ CB page 33

About the exam:
In the exam, you have to complete eight gaps in a text. You have to make a new word from the one given in capitals at the end of some of the lines.

Strategy:
• Read the title and the whole text first for meaning.
• Look at each gap in the text and decide if you need, e.g. a noun, adjective, verb or adverb.
• Look at the word in capitals and decide how to make it fit the gap.
• These changes may be made by adding a prefix or suffix, making a change in the middle of the word (*foot → feet*) or making a compound word (*feed → feedback*).
• Remember, you don't need to make more than two changes to the word.

1 Look at the suffixes and examples. Match suffixes 1–6 with meanings A–F.

1	-ous	fam**ous**, danger**ous**
2	-er/-or	teach**er**, act**or**
3	-less	home**less**, care**less**
4	-ive	attract**ive**, creat**ive**
5	-ly	quick**ly**, thoughtful**ly**
6	-able	drink**able**, count**able**

A having the character of
B without
C capable of being
D full of
E how something is done
F someone who

2 Use the word given in capitals at the end of the line to form a noun that fits in the gap in the same line.

PLAYING THE PIANO: FROM BAD TO GOOD

I've played the piano since I was five. I had no interest in learning a **(0)** _musical_ instrument – it was my mum who decided it was a good idea. **MUSIC**

I went to lessons every week. My friends thought it was really **(1)** .... and I hated it. I wanted to be outside riding my bike like them. Then, my mum started entering me for **(2)** .... I think she had an idea that I might one day become a **(3)** .... musician! Everyone else seemed to be **(4)** .... to be taking part but I never won anything. I was completely **(5)** .... and it was awful. **USUAL COMPETE FAME EXCITE HOPE**

Now I'm an adult, I'm glad my mum made me practise for hours because I feel more **(6)** .... playing in front of people. I actually find playing for my friends great fun and I really like to be **(7)** .... when I play. But if I ever have **(8)** ...., I'll let them do whatever they want! **COMFORT CREATE CHILD**

Writing
Review ▶ CB page 34

About the exam:
In the exam, you choose between different tasks. One of the options may be a review of a book, a film, a play, a place or a product. You need to write **140–190** words.

Strategy:
- It doesn't matter if you like or dislike what you are reviewing, but give examples for your opinion.
- Include general information, say why you liked/disliked it and make a recommendation.
- Use an informal style.

1 Read the exam task and the answer. Then complete the review with the words in the box.

> You recently saw this notice on a magazine website.
> *Have you seen a good documentary recently? What was special about it? Send us your review and we'll post the three best ones on the website.*
> Write a review in **140–190** words.

awards   came   combines   ever   follows
found   remarkable   seem

Man on Wire

I enjoy documentaries and one of the most interesting I've **(1)** .... seen is the British-made *Man on Wire*, which **(2)** .... out in 2008. It won many **(3)** .... at the time.

Man on Wire **(4)** .... the real story of Robert Petit, a French tightrope walker. Robert developed a particular obsession when he was ten years old. In 1974, his dream finally came true. He walked across a wire stretched between the Twin Towers in New York, 1,350 feet up in the air, not just once, but eight times!

The first **(5)** .... thing about this documentary is how the director **(6)** .... real film and photographs from 1974 with current interviews. The second is that the documentary is filmed like a crime film. As the team plan to enter the Towers illegally it is just like the planning for a bank robbery!

I **(7)** .... this documentary fascinating, funny and entertaining. It's amazing to see how a dream can come true, however impossible it may **(8)** ....!

2 Make notes for a review of a documentary you have seen. Organise the points into paragraphs and then write the review in your notebook.

A sense of adventure

Reading

Multiple choice ▶ CB pages 38–39

1 **Read the article on page 25 quickly and choose the correct answers.**

1 Where was the research boat?

   A near South America **B** near South Korea **C** near South Africa

2 How big was the shark?

   A three metres **B** three and a half metres **C** five metres

3 What happened to the shark?

   A it died **B** it was taken to a research centre
   C it was put back in the sea

2 **Match words 1–6 with meanings A–F.**

1 tow   **A** unable to find a way out
2 bait   **B** small animals that big animals hunt for food
3 trapped   **C** people who work on a boat
4 rope   **D** use a vehicle to pull something
5 prey   **E** food used to attract animals
6 crew   **F** thick line used to tie things

3 **Read the article again and choose the answer (A, B or C) which you think fits best.**

1 The writer suggests that many people

   A know a lot about marine biology.

   B enjoy reading about marine research projects.

   C would like the same experiences as marine researchers.

2 The scientists were in the boat because they wanted to

   A catch some sharks.

   B observe the sharks' behaviour.

   C talk to the fishermen in the area.

3 What were the scientists doing when the shark jumped?

   A They were putting some food in the water.

   B They were watching sharks swimming by the boat.

   C They were waiting quietly.

4 What did the shark do when it landed on the boat?

   A It fell on and crushed a crew member.

   B It broke some things on the boat.

   C It prevented the men from moving.

5 After the first rescue, the shark had difficulty

   A getting free from the ropes.

   B using its tail to swim.

   C finding the open sea.

6 How does Gennari, a shark expert, feel about the event?

   A sure that the shark did not intend to jump on the boat

   B worried that the shark might attack again

   C amazed that it could jump so high

4 **Complete the collocations with words from the article.**

1 I think writers .... very interesting *lives*.

2 We're going to .... *a survey* at school to find out who has had the most exciting holiday.

3 When the cruise liner was in port we *went* .... *board* and had a look round. It was amazing!

4 We couldn't see the performers on stage so we *pushed our* .... to the front of the audience.

5 We rescued a bird with a broken wing and helped .... *it alive* by giving it some bread before we took it to the vet.

6 Janine *had a* .... *escape* last week when her bike nearly went into a river!

Great white shark jumps from sea into research boat

Marine researchers lead an interesting and exciting life. They do important work and visit places all round the world that normal people can only dream of. They find and observe animals and plants that most of us only ever see on TV and in books. However, life became a little more exciting than expected for some scientists in the sea off the coast of South Africa recently.

Several scientists were conducting a survey of the shark population when they suddenly got much closer to a shark than they wanted! The scientists were on board a research boat called *Cheetah* and they were putting sardines into the water to attract white sharks. These wonderful animals are known to jump out of the water when they see some prey. The scientists wanted to watch this type of activity.

Dorien Schröder is the team leader at Oceans Research. She said that after more than an hour of shark activity around the boat, the waters at the front of the boat had been quiet for five minutes. 'Next thing I know, I hear a loud splash, and see a white shark jump out of the water directly over the man who was throwing sardines into the sea!'

Schröder pulled her colleague to safety before the shark, weighing about 500kg (half a ton) and about three metres long, landed on top of the bait and fuel containers. It was about three metres long! At first, half of its body was outside the boat but in a panic the shark pushed its way further on to *Cheetah*. It cut fuel lines and smashed equipment before becoming trapped between the containers and the back of the boat. The crew ran to the front of the boat for safety.

Schröder poured water over the shark to keep it alive, and the crew tied a rope round the shark's tail. A second boat then towed *Cheetah* to the port with the shark still on deck. Eventually, the big fish was lifted off by machinery and then lowered back into the water.

Though the shark swam away it was unable to find its way out of the harbour and soon ended up on the beach. With Oceans Research's co-director, Enrico Gennari, an expert on great white sharks, the team tried many ways to rescue the animal. Finally, they used ropes to pull it through the harbour and back out to sea. The ropes were then removed and the animal swam away.

Gennari said it was the first time he had heard of a great white shark jumping onto a research boat. He guessed that the animal had jumped about three metres out of the water to be able to land on the boat. As for the cause of the shark's behaviour, Gennari said it was almost certainly an accident and not an attack on the boat. In the dark water the big fish might have thought that the boat's shadow was prey. 'It's all speculation,' he said. 'But sometimes a shark jumps out of the water when it feels another shark underneath it. They move like a flying fish and end up several metres away.'

In this case, both scientists and shark had a narrow escape. But there can't be many scientists who have had the chance to get so close to a great white shark. And there can't be many sharks that have got so close to their observers!

Grammar

narrative tenses ▶ CB page 40

1 **Match 1–6 with A–F to complete a story.**

1 It was a great day for snowboarding.

2 I had got all my gear ready the night before,

3 The slopes had just opened when

4 I was speeding down the mountain on my board when

5 I couldn't see what it was but

6 It was a huge white swan flying over the slopes!

A so I set off to the mountains nice and early.

B It flew over my head and into the distance. What a strange sight!

C I saw something in the air ahead of me.

D I arrived.

E it was coming towards me very quickly!

F The sun was shining and the snow was fresh.

2 **Complete the text with the past simple, past continuous or past perfect simple form of the verbs in brackets.**

time phrases ▶ CB page 40

3 **Cross out the alternative(s) which are NOT possible to complete the sentences.**

1 *Afterwards/As soon as/When* I reached the hotel, I went for a swim in the pool.

2 *While/When/As soon as* Sue had booked the travel arrangements, she rang to tell me.

3 Michael cooked dinner for Petra *after/when/by the time* she got home from her trip.

4 *While/During/After* the sun was going down, we sipped cocktails on the balcony.

5 I was really hungry *by the time/afterwards/when* I had finished skiing.

6 *During/While/When* Jay was collecting the luggage, he dropped a suitcase on his toe.

7 The flight was so tiring that *as soon as/by the time/when* I got home, I went to bed and slept for twelve hours.

8 *During/When/While* my trip to Morocco I went to see the city of Casablanca.

BLOG ▶

A party in Oporto

What a trip I had last month! My friend, Noela, **(1)** .... (*invite*) me to her 21st birthday in Oporto, Portugal. She studied English with me in London last summer and we had stayed in touch. This was a chance to see her again and I **(2)** .... (*look forward to*) it. I **(3)** .... (*book*) my flights and accommodation, found a great outfit to wear and bought a cool gift for Noela.

On the day of the party, everything was going really well. I **(4)** .... (*arrive*) in Oporto the night before, the weather was beautiful and I was really excited to be in a city I **(5)** .... (*never go*) to before. I set off from my hostel in the direction of the hotel where the party was taking place. I got onto the tram and **(6)** .... (*look*) at the map of the city in my guidebook when I had a sudden feeling that I **(7)** .... (*go*) in the wrong direction!

I quickly got off the tram and looked around. Then I **(8)** .... (*realise*) I was lost in a strange city without knowing a word of Portuguese! Fortunately, a very kind girl saw me looking at my map and she asked me in English where I wanted to go. I **(9)** .... (*explain*) the situation and then she smiled and pointed across the road. I **(10)** .... (*stand*) opposite the hotel! I had been going in the right direction after all!

Speaking

Long turn ▶ CB page 41

1 ▶06 **Listen to the question then complete a candidate's comments about the pictures with the words in the box.**

| if | imagine | looks | might | probably | sure |

1 The people in the second picture are .... at an airport.
2 I .... the people at the airport are feeling pretty fed up.
3 It looks as .... the people in the first picture are trying to get on an underground train.
4 It .... be during the rush hour.
5 One person at least .... really tired.
6 I'm .... it's really boring to wait for ages like that.

2 ▶07 **Listen to follow-up questions 1–3 and match with answers A–C.**

A At a train station, because it's more crowded and usually there is more to do at an airport.

B It's OK, but I sometimes get a bit scared when we take off and land.

C Yes, I love it. It's quick and easy and it's fun to watch all the people.

Listening

Multiple choice ▶ CB page 42

1 ▶08 **Listen to a radio interview with an author and answer the questions.**

1 What is the name of the book? ....
2 Where did the event Monty describes happen? ....
3 Did the man live or die? ....

2 ▶08 **Listen to the interview again. For questions 1–5, choose the best answer, A, B or C.**

1 Why did Monty write the book?
A He saw an interesting film.
B He was in a small plane crash.
C Someone told him a great story.
2 The man was found by two people
A whose car had broken down.
B who were travelling in the area.
C who were searching for someone else.
3 Monty thinks the man was in the car because he
A was upset because of personal relationships.
B had had an accident.
C was confused by the roads.
4 His survival was probably helped because
A he built an igloo round his car.
B the temperatures stayed above freezing.
C he was able to cover himself warmly.
5 What do doctors disagree about?
A how long people can live without food and water
B whether people can hibernate like animals when it's cold
C what people can learn from studying animal behaviour

Vocabulary

extreme adjectives ▶ CB page 43

1 Find the extremes of the adjectives in the box in the wordsearch below.

bad big cold hot hungry interesting
loud scary small tired

T	D	O	D	I	K	V	A	N	N	O	T
S	T	F	R	E	E	Z	I	N	G	C	X
S	E	E	X	H	A	U	S	T	E	D	E
C	J	T	R	T	R	F	P	S	E	K	R
F	Z	S	V	R	I	I	E	E	P	E	D
S	T	A	R	V	I	N	G	N	R	E	B
J	E	J	E	R	D	F	Y	C	I	O	S
T	X	O	F	A	H	J	Y	F	O	N	B
F	A	S	C	I	N	A	T	I	N	G	G
T	E	R	R	I	B	L	E	E	N	A	E
E	N	O	R	M	O	U	S	J	P	G	C
A	X	I	N	U	B	O	I	L	I	N	G

2 Complete the sentences with the correct adjectives from the wordsearch.

1 When the tree crashed down in our garden the noise was ....

2 I hadn't eaten all day and I was .... by the time I got to the hotel.

3 It was a lovely meal but it cost my parents an .... amount of money.

4 The bus driver drove very dangerously and for me the whole journey was ....!

5 The temperatures dropped a lot overnight and in the morning it was ....

6 I have a scar on my hand because of the accident but you can hardly see it, it's so ....

Grammar

subject/object questions ▶ CB page 44

1 Read the news story. Then choose the correct alternatives for the questions 1–6.

All's well that ends well

Jake and Sarah Mellor have just returned from what should have been a sunny, romantic getaway. Jake had planned to ask Sarah to marry him once they had arrived at a luxury hotel in the romantic Indian city of Udaipur. But Jake hadn't done his research properly and the couple arrived in the middle of the monsoon season! The weather was absolutely terrible! Poor Jake's plans of getting down on one knee outside one of the city's beautiful palaces suddenly didn't seem like such a good idea in the pouring rain.

But Jake wasn't a person to give in easily and he approached the manager of the hotel they were staying in to ask if the chef could prepare a special meal with a diamond engagement ring hidden inside it for his wife-to-be. Of course, the hotel manager was happy to help Jake and promised a fabulous dinner in the restaurant overlooking a nearby lake.

The meal arrived and Sarah was enjoying the delicious food when she suddenly bit on something hard. 'I thought I had broken a tooth!' she laughed. 'But when I saw the ring and Jake asked me to marry him, I said yes straightaway.' The couple plan to get married in a palace in Udaipur – in the dry season of course!

1 A Where did Jake and Sarah go on holiday?
  B Where Jake and Sarah went on holiday?

2 A Where the couple did stay in the city?
  B Where did the couple stay in the city?

3 A What Jake planned to do?
  B What did Jake plan to do?

4 A Who did Jake ask to help him?
  B Who asked Jake to help him?

5 A Who cooked a special meal?
  B Who did cook a special meal?

6 A What Sarah did think she broke?
  B What did Sarah think she had broken?

2 Match answers A–F with questions 1–6 in Activity 1.

A the hotel manager ....

B Udaipur ....

C ask Sarah to marry him ....

D in a luxury hotel ....

E a tooth ....

F the hotel chef ....

Use of English

Key word transformations
▶ CB page 45

1 **Complete the second sentence so that it has a similar meaning to the first sentence, using the word given. You must use between two and five words, including the word given.**

1 I think it's going to rain.

AS It .... going to rain.

2 My dad became a pilot ten years ago.

FOR My dad .... ten years.

3 I hurt my leg during the football match today.

WHILE I hurt my leg ....
football today.

4 It was extremely cold when we were in Scotland.

ABSOLUTELY It .... when we
were in Scotland.

5 Mark arrived late so we missed the bus.

UP Mark .... we missed the
bus.

6 In my opinion, the exhibition was fascinating.

FOUND I .... fascinating.

Writing

Report ▶ CB page 46

1 **Read the exam task. Which of the points below do you think should NOT be included in the report?**

> Your teacher has asked you to write a report on safety and security at your college for new students. You should explain fire and accident procedures and advise how to protect personal property.

1 Students shouldn't come to college if they've got a cold.

2 There is a fire drill every week.

3 Students shouldn't leave money in the classrooms.

4 There is a student car park.

5 Smoking is allowed in the College gardens.

6 There are vegetarian meals in the cafeteria.

2 **Read the answer and check your ideas.**

Introduction
[1]The aim of this report is to give information to new students about college safety and security.

Fire
There are instructions in each classroom about what to do if there is a fire, which you should read carefully, and we have a weekly fire drill. [2]You should find out where the fire exits are.

Accidents
If you have an accident or feel ill, there is a nurse's room on Floor 3. Any accidents in the college [3]must be reported and recorded in the 'Accident Book' in Reception.

Security
[4]We advise you not to bring a lot of money or expensive things to College. [5]Our advice is to take bags or laptops with you when you leave the classroom. If necessary, you can lock valuable items in the Principal's safe.

Conclusion
[6]Generally speaking, the College is a safe and secure place. Let's keep it this way.

3 **Which of the phrases A–F could replace the underlined phrases 1–6 in the report?**

A It's important to …	D The purpose …
B You shouldn't …	E On the whole …
C We recommend taking …	F should be written …

4 **Read the exam task. Make notes and write your report. Write 140–190 words.**

> Your teacher has asked you to write a report for new students on safety and security at the swimming pool in your college. You should explain safety and accident procedures, and give advice on how to protect personal property.

The consumer society

5

Vocabulary

shops and shopping ▶ CB pages 48–49

1 **Read the clues and complete the crossword.**

Across

1 People usually do this in shops when they don't particularly want to buy something.
2 Name of a product or group of products made by a company.
3 People use this when they don't want to pay for something immediately.
4 A small image that represents a company.
5 You can buy and sell things at these places, usually outside.
6 A store which is part of a bigger group of shops run by the same company.
7 An area where lots of shops are together.

Down

1 Something you buy cheaply.

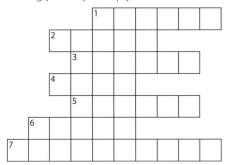

2 **Complete the blog extract with the correct form of the words from Activity 1. One word is used twice.**

I must admit, I'm a bit of a shopaholic! I love all sorts of shopping, whether it's in a shopping **(1)** .... or an outside street **(2)** .... and I especially like looking for **(3)** ....! Whenever there's a sale advertised, I'm there! Sometimes I just **(4)** .... but other times I spend way too much. But I try not to buy things on **(5)** .... because I don't like being in debt and often if I haven't got much money I check out the **(6)** .... things in charity shops. You can often get good **(7)** .... when you buy designer items there. Mind you, I'm not that worried about having a famous **(8)** .... on everything I buy. Just one Ralph Lauren T-shirt or pair of Jimmy Choo shoes is fine with me!

Listening
Multiple choice ▶ CB page 49

1 ▶ 09 **Listen to people talking in different situations. Match recordings 1–5 with situations A–E.**

A You hear a customer making a complaint. ....

B You hear two friends talking about a shirt one of them has bought. ....

C You hear part of a news report about the way people shop. ....

D You hear two people talking about designer clothes. ....

E You hear a girl talking to her friend about saving money. ....

2 ▶ 09 **Listen again and answer the questions by choosing A, B or C.**

1 What is the boy doing?
 A asking for help
 B admitting a mistake
 C accepting advice

2 What do they agree about designer clothes?
 A They are good quality.
 B They are not worth the money.
 C They are expensive because of the name.

3 What does she want the sales assistant to do?
 A give her a refund for the shoes
 B exchange the shoes
 C give her a discount on another pair of shoes

4 What does the man say about consumers?
 A They are refusing to give up luxury items.
 B They are finding new places to shop.
 C They are avoiding buying food on the internet.

5 Why does the boy think the girl's plans are unrealistic?
 A She will not be able to stop going out.
 B She will never afford to buy a car.
 C She will become bored with her clothes.

Grammar
future forms ▶ CB page 50

1 **Cross out the option that is NOT possible in each sentence.**

1 *I'm taking/I'm going to take/I take* that new phone back to the shop this morning – it isn't working properly.

2 *I'll meet/I'm meeting/I'm going to meet* Tina at the leather market at 3 p.m. She wants to buy a new bag.

3 Where do you think *I'm getting/I might get/I'll get* the best deal on a second-hand car?

4 Oh no! The website's crashed on the payments page. *I'll have to/I'm having to/I'm going to have to* start again!

5 I think *I'll look at/I look at/I might look at* some of those price comparison websites for travel insurance later. It depends how tired I am after work.

6 The bank *might close/closes/will close* at 4 p.m., so I'd better go and pay the money in now.

2 **Complete the text with *might*, *will*, *going to* or the present continuous. Use the verb in brackets. Sometimes more than one future form is possible.**

Hi, Charlie!

What **(1)** .... (*do*) this evening? I'm **(2)** .... (*go*) shopping. It's my twin brother and sister's birthday on Sunday. I've got lots to buy, so I'm going into town after my classes.

I **(3)** .... (*buy*) my sister a voucher and for my brother, an alarm clock – he loves his gadgets! I think they'll be really pleased with those.

After shopping, I **(4)** .... (*meet*) my friends and we **(5)** .... (*have*) dinner at our favourite pizza restaurant. One of my friends, Steph, hasn't been before but I'm sure she **(6)** .... (*like*) it. Then we **(7)** .... (*go*) to see a late-night film at the cinema which starts at 11 p.m., but it depends how tired we are!

I **(8)** .... (*write*) again soon.

Love,

Elena

Speaking
Collaborative task ▶ CB page 51

1 **Complete the comments about organising an event to raise money for charity with the words in the box.**

about   agree   could   don't   Let's   might
sure   work

1 .... have a big sale of second-hand items for charity.

2 We .... always ask the teachers to donate some things for the sale.

3 What do you think .... asking a local celebrity to come too?

4 It .... be better to have it in summer when the weather's sunny.

5 Why .... we sell sandwiches and soft drinks too?

6 That might .... but we need to organise it carefully.

7 I'm not too .... .There are a lot of sales like this these days.

8 But don't you .... that everyone loves a bargain? We'll make a lot of money.

2 **Which two phrases underlined in Activity 1 are responses to suggestions?**

3 ▶ 10 **Read the exam task and choose the correct words to complete the phrases. Then listen and check.**

> I'd like you to imagine that your school is having a big sale of second-hand items to raise money for charity. Here are some ways they could advertise the sale.

A: So, let's think about leaflets first. Is that a good way of advertising? What do you think?

B: Mmm. They're quite quick and easy to do – and they won't cost too much. But don't you think that a lot of people will just throw them away?

A: I know what you **(1)** *say/mean*. If you get a leaflet, you often don't even look at it! Especially if it comes through the door.

B: How about a radio commercial? Loads of people listen to the radio.

A: You're **(2)** *OK/right*. Dad always has it on in his car. But it might be a bit expensive.

B: It **(3)** *depends/can*. We could always record it ourselves – we wouldn't have to pay actors!

A: And that **(4)** *shall/would* be great fun! OK – that's a possibility. Then, of course, there are posters. I'm sure the school could produce those.

B: And we **(5)** *might/could* go round sticking them up in shop windows. People usually look at posters – particularly if they're bright and clever. The art students could design some good ones.

A: Cool! And the newsletter advert would be good. It won't cost anything.

B: Yeah. But it only goes to school students and families, doesn't it? We need to get to a wider audience.

A: So, **(6)** *could/maybe* the advert in the local paper is a good idea. People often browse through the 'What's on?' section when it gets near the weekend.

B: Good **(7)** *thought/idea*. How about the T-shirts? I really like the idea – but it would cost a lot.

A: But **(8)** *while/then* if all the organisers wear a T-shirt advertising the sale for a few weeks before, people will notice, won't they?

B: I'm not too sure **(9)** *on/about* that. It will only really be their friends and family and they'll know anyway! I think you just want a free T-shirt!

A: (laughs) Why **(10)** *not/so*?!

leaflets and fliers

radio advert

posters in shop windows

How effective might these forms of advertising be?

school newsletter

T-shirts advertising the sale

advert in local newspaper

Examiner: Now you have a minute to decide which form of advertising should not be used.

Reading

Gapped text ▶ CB pages 52–53

1 **Read the title of the article. What does *swapped* mean?**

1 bought ☐

2 exchanged ☐

2 **Read the article and choose from sentences A–G the one which fits each gap. There is one extra sentence which you do not need to use.**

A From the start, MacDonald insisted on meeting each person with whom he was dealing.

B I don't see it as any more strange than offering your time in return for a salary like most people in full-time jobs do.

C 'I was doing trades all over the place without spending any of my own money on petrol or plane fares,' he said.

D However, no one seems more surprised by his success than Kyle himself.

E This was even more remarkable as MacDonald had intended the whole thing to be 'just a bit of fun'.

F 'I only dealt with people I liked the sound of, or who seemed to genuinely support the idea of the website.'

G Why not see what people would give him in exchange for it?

3 **Match the underlined words in the article with the meanings 1–6.**

1 very strange ....

2 with no value ....

3 useful ....

4 looked quickly ....

5 simple and different work ....

6 not important ....

I swapped my paper clip for a house …

Do you, like me, have a drawer somewhere at home full of different bits of rubbish which you think might come in <u>handy</u> some day? If so, the story of Canadian internet entrepreneur Kyle MacDonald may inspire you to take a closer look at what is hiding among the old pieces of paper and bits of string.

A few years ago, Kyle set out on what seemed at the time a ridiculous and impossible project – to trade a single red paper clip for a house. He advertised this almost <u>worthless</u> item on the internet and succeeded in swapping it for bigger and better things. Twelve months and thirteen swaps later, he announced that his final deal had got him a property, a two-storey farmhouse in Kipling, Saskatchewan. **[1]** It certainly turned out to be more than that!

Kyle graduated with a degree in geography before travelling the world. He did <u>odd jobs</u> – from delivering pizzas to working on oil rigs. One day, he received an email from an old friend reminding him of a game called *Bigger and Better* which they had played as children. In this game, you started with small objects and competed to see what you could trade them for. MacDonald finished reading the email, <u>glanced</u> down at his desk and saw a red paper clip. **[2]** And so a strange and brilliant idea was born.

He wrote down this ambition. 'I'm going to keep trading up until I get a house,' he wrote. His first offer was a pen in the shape of a fish. This was soon exchanged for a doorknob with a smiley face and the doorknob, in turn, for an outdoor stove. **[3]** It was, he says, 'just a great way to meet new people'.

In this, he did have some help. His father, an enthusiastic inventor, had come up with a new idea for restaurant tables. MacDonald travelled across America and Canada to advertise his father's product. On the way, he would stop off to meet the people who'd contacted him on his website and who he wanted to do business with on his paper clip project. **[4]**

As news of the website spread, MacDonald had to choose between hundreds of offers for each item he advertised but he says their financial value was <u>irrelevant</u>. **[5]** Kyle continued to trade up. His trades included an appearance on TV, some time in a recording studio, an afternoon with the rock star Alice Cooper and a small role in a film. Finally he got his house.

Kyle tries to explain his success. 'People might think this is an <u>odd</u> way to spend your time but remember that before money was invented people swapped things for centuries. **[6]**

What's that blue plastic object on my desk? It is the top of an old pen. Once I might have thrown it in the bin but now I pick it up and turn it thoughtfully in my fingers. Today, it's just a plastic pen top … tomorrow it could be a villa in Tuscany.

Grammar

be used to/get used to ▶ CB page 54

1 Complete the text with the positive or negative forms of *be used to* and *get used to*.

I'm from Spain and I came to live in the UK a few months ago. I'm a shopaholic and I *love* shopping! But it's taken me a while to **(1)** .... shopping here. I live in a village and the shops close at 5.30 p.m. I **(2)** .... that because in Spain they're open much later and I **(3)** .... being able to go shopping after work. I can't do that now, so I have to either shop online or wait until the weekend. One thing I **(4)** .... is the prices because they're much higher in the UK. It's taken me ages to **(5)** .... shopping without comparing how much I'd spend on a similar item back home. The sizes are different too, so I can't just walk into a shop and pick something up without trying it like I **(6)** .... !

2 Find and correct the mistakes in the sentences 1–6. There is one mistake in each sentence.

1 I still haven't got used to get up so early for my new job.

2 Sue didn't think she'd like living on her own but she used to it now.

3 I got used to do all my shopping online when I moved to a small village.

4 Antonio said it is too difficult to be used to the British weather so he's going back to Portugal.

5 Jen is used to getting so much attention from the media. It's all new to her and she hates it.

6 It took me ages to be used to living in a big city but I love it now.

Use of English

Multiple-choice cloze ▶ CB page 55

1 Match words 1–6 with the parts of speech A–F.

1	customer	A	adjective
2	therefore	B	adverb
3	quickly	C	linking word
4	down	D	preposition
5	expensive	E	verb
6	spend	F	noun

2 Read the article and decide which answer (A, B, C or D) best fits each gap.

Supermarket scams

Supermarkets are very **(0)** *good* at deceiving their poor customers, it seems. Customers, **(1)** .... think they are getting good value for money, are **(2)** .... getting less of a bargain than they imagine. **(3)** .... are a couple of the most common tricks used by supermarkets to keep their customers spending.

You might think that buying a bigger packet would cost you quite a lot less, right? Wrong. At Superco, for example, a 100g jar of coffee costs £3.00. **(4)** ...., a 200g jar costs £5.99 – a saving of **(5)** .... one penny!

Special offers. You've seen them on the shelves – 'buy one, get one free'. The best offers are usually on fruit and vegetables – but can you *really* eat **(6)** .... those potatoes before they go bad and you have to throw them **(7)** .... ?

So, **(8)** .... to think about what you're buying before you fill up your shopping trolley!

0	**A** good	**B** well	**C** fine	**D** right
1	**A** what	**B** who	**C** when	**D** where
2	**A** absolutely	**B** exactly	**C** actually	**D** correctly
3	**A** Here	**B** There	**C** This	**D** Now
4	**A** Although	**B** Whereas	**C** Because	**D** However
5	**A** only	**B** almost	**C** around	**D** about
6	**A** every	**B** all	**C** most	**D** some
7	**A** up	**B** around	**C** off	**D** away
8	**A** forget	**B** avoid	**C** remind	**D** remember

Writing
Essay ▶ CB page 56

1 **When you are writing an essay, are statements 1–5 *true* (T) or *false* (F)?**

1 You should agree with the statement in the exam task.

2 It is better to write a lot of short sentences than longer, more complex ones.

3 It is a good idea to give examples for both points of view.

4 In your conclusion, you should repeat what you say in the introduction.

5 It's a good idea to have one long paragraph.

2 **Read the exam task and the answer. Complete the essay with the correct words.**

> In class you have been discussing money and happiness. Your teacher has now asked you to write an essay. Write an essay using all the notes and give reasons for your point of view.
>
> **Essay question:**
> *Does buying lots of things make you happy?*
>
> **Notes:**
>
> Things to write about:
>
> 1 health
> 2 security
> 3 your own idea.
>
> Write your essay in **140–190** words.

all   balance   course   However   view   well

In the past, people usually bought things because they needed them. Now, we spend money on things that we want, not on things that we need. We buy things because we think they will make us happy. But do they?

First of **(1)** .... , I must say that money can make us happy in many ways. Of **(2)** .... , it can stop us worrying about a lot of the important things in life, such as having somewhere to live and keeping warm. As **(3)** .... as this, it can help us enjoy our free time by buying concert or theatre tickets or gym membership.

(4) .... , many people think material things are too important. In my **(5)** .... , money cannot buy us friends or good health. What is more, I really believe that it is immoral to spend our money on luxury items when many people in the world are so poor they cannot afford basic medicine.

On **(6)** .... , I think material things can help us to be happy but there are many more things in life that we should think about rather than just buying things all the time.

3 **Match the underlined phrases in the essay with words and phrases 1–6.**

1 On the whole ....
2 Obviously ....
3 As far as I'm concerned ....
4 To begin with ....
5 Nevertheless ....
6 In addition to this ....

4 **Read the exam task and write your answer.**

> You have recently had a discussion in your class about money. Your teacher has now asked you to write an essay.
>
> Write an essay using all the notes.
>
> **Essay question:**
> *Is it better to save money or spend it?*
>
> **Notes:**
>
> Things to write about:
>
> 1 enjoyment
> 2 security
> 3 your own idea
>
> Write your essay in **140–190** words.

Working lives

Vocabulary

finding a job ▶ CB pages 58–59

1 **Choose the correct alternative to complete the sentences.**

1 A job should give you *a sense/an emotion* of achievement that makes you feel that you've done well.

2 Ambitious people look for a job that has good *ambitions/prospects* so that they can advance quickly.

3 However much you love your job, I think you need to find a good work–life *balance/similarity* or you miss out on some important things.

4 I need a *fully/well*-paid job because I have to pay a lot for my accommodation.

5 My mum gave up her *complete/full*-time job when she had a family and went part-time for several years.

6 Could you please send me a(n) *applying/application* form for the job advertised in the paper?

2 **Match words 1–8 with definitions A–H.**

1	secure	A	not temporary
2	status	B	money for a job paid weekly
3	rewarding	C	not likely to change, you can depend on it
4	salary	D	a formal meeting for someone to ask you questions
5	stressful	E	money usually paid for a job every month
6	interview	F	important position
7	permanent	G	giving a lot of satisfaction
8	wage	H	causing a lot of worry

3 **Complete the email with words from Activity 2.**

Hi, Brad

I've really got to find a new job – one that's a bit less **(1)** .... than this one! I seem to be worrying all the time. Do you know of any job vacancies locally? I'm looking for something **(2)** .... – obviously I want a job that I can depend on, at least for a few months. But it doesn't have to be **(3)** .... or long term. Money isn't a big concern for me so I don't need a high monthly **(4)** .... but I'd really like to do something that's **(5)** .... and that motivates me. I had an **(6)** .... for a job at a restaurant last week, but I haven't heard back from them. So any suggestions would be good!

Thanks!

Mick

Speaking
Collaborative task and discussion
▶ CB page 59

1 ▶ **11 Read the exam task and listen to a conversation between two candidates. Then answer the questions.**

> Here are some people who do jobs that are sometimes dangerous. Talk together about how dangerous you think these jobs are. Now decide which job is the most rewarding.

1 Which job do they NOT discuss?

2 Do they do everything they are asked in the task?

wildlife photographer

top chef in a restaurant

firefighter

police officer

high-rise building window cleaner

2 ▶ **11 Listen again and tick the comments the candidates make.**

1 Chefs can get health problems. ☐

2 Firefighters get good salaries. ☐

3 Photographers often get attacked. ☐

4 Window cleaners need to have good equipment. ☐

5 Police officers have a long training. ☐

6 People often complain about police officers. ☐

About the exam:

In Part 4 of the exam, you will be asked some questions related to the topic of your Part 3 discussion. You will need to give your opinions. You will be asked between 2 and 4 questions. Sometimes you will be encouraged to give your opinion on a question your partner has answered.

Strategy:

Try to give a full answer with your reasons and perhaps an example from your experience. You can add your opinion after your partner has answered and this can develop into a discussion.

3 **Match questions 1–5 with answers A–E. Then complete the answers with the phrases in the box.**

> It all   I've never thought
> That's an interesting   To be   to think of it

1 Do you think that people usually follow their parents and do the same job as they do?

2 Do you think it's a good idea for schools to invite people who do different jobs to talk to their students?

3 Do you think that people who do dangerous jobs should be paid a lot of money?

4 Would you like to do a dangerous job?

5 What do you think makes people do dangerous jobs?

A .... question. I'm not really sure. Some people should get paid more if the danger is very high, and they're doing things to save people's lives. But if it's a choice – like the photographer – then no, not really.

B .... depends. Sometimes people see their parents doing a job that they love and they think, yes, I'd like to do that too. But not always.

C .... honest, I can't understand why some people choose to do things like that. I could never work high up like those people! Maybe they enjoy the fear?

D .... about it before. I suppose it depends how much I needed the money! I couldn't see myself cooking in a hot kitchen, though!

E Come ...., that might be a good idea. I think children would enjoy listening to people like that at school. It would help them choose a good job too.

Reading
Multiple matching   ▶ CB pages 60–61

1 You are going to read a magazine article about people who turned their hobbies into jobs. Read the article quickly and decide if the statements are *true* (T) or *false* (F).

1 All the people are happy about what they have done.
....

2 All the people found it hard to turn their hobby into a job. ....

2 Read the magazine article about people who turned their hobbies into jobs. For questions 1–10, choose from people A–C. The people may be chosen more than once.

Which person

had to improve their skills in a new area quickly? `1`

was uncertain about how attractive their product was? `2`

made a decision not to do something they had planned? `3`

found it difficult to build up their work? `4`

did something they realised was wrong? `5`

received positive comments about what they made? `6`

has moved on from their first role in their new career? `7`

was surprised that their hobby turned into a job? `8`

developed a love for their work from someone else? `9`

says they are lucky to have a satisfying career? `10`

3 Match the underlined words and phrases in the article with definitions 1–6.

1 try extremely hard to achieve something difficult   ....
2 satisfactory   ....
3 reply   ....
4 test   ....
5 became very interested in   ....
6 someone with a lot of skill in a subject   ....

How my hobby became my job

Three people tell features reporter Sue Carter how they turned their hobbies into full-time careers.

A Computer games inventor

When I was at school, I never used to pay attention in IT classes – not because I was bored but because I loved seeing what I could do on the computer. I'd play around on it when I was supposed to be doing my classwork. It was a bit naughty I know, but it's how I came up with the idea for a new computer game. I got my friends to try it out at break times and they loved it. I wasn't sure whether other people would like it, though so I decided to put it on a gaming site and see if I'd get any <u>response</u>. To my amazement, I did. People started messaging me about how much they liked it and suddenly everyone wanted to have a go. I couldn't believe that what started as me playing around at school became a real job, selling my game online. Eventually I was developing games full-time and my new ones are becoming just as popular. I know some people <u>struggle</u> to find work that they enjoy, so I'm fortunate that my favourite hobby has also become my job.

B Jewellery maker

I've always been into making things. My grandma loved knitting and I remember watching her make tiny outfits for my dolls when I was young. Then, when I was a little older, she taught me to knit myself and there was no stopping me. I used to make crazy clothes that were the envy of all my friends. Then I started work in a busy office and didn't really have time to do what I loved most. My job wasn't creative at all and I was disappointed not to be fulfilling that side of me. That's when I decided to learn something new and I went to a jewellery-making workshop. Immediately, I was hooked and I made loads of earrings and necklaces. I would give them to friends as gifts and it was my best friend, Nancy, who said I should try selling them. I set up a little online shop and got some good feedback from my new customers. It was slow and very hard work but I've managed to establish a business that provides me with a decent income and I love my new job!

C Kiteboarding instructor

I've spent my life in the water and I was first hired as a sailing instructor when I was eighteen in the summer before going to university, just as a holiday job. They had just started offering kiteboarding and I loved the idea of having a go at teaching it. I'd taught myself the summer before by getting out on the sea with a board and kite. Luckily for me, I picked it up straight away. The sport became really popular at the centre and I loved my job so much that I made up my mind to stay on there full-time rather than go to university. I soon became an expert and found myself working on a watersports magazine as an editor and gave up teaching the sport. This meant I had plenty of free time to travel and try out new places to do kiteboarding. I sometimes wonder what I'd be doing now if I'd gone to university but I love what I do and there's no going back.

Grammar

making comparisons ▶ CB page 62

1 **Choose the correct option to complete the sentences.**

1 Sheila works *more slow/slower* than Lin but her work is more accurate.
2 Andula is a tree surgeon. She says it's the *most dangerous/dangerous* job she's ever had.
3 Charlie works the *longest/longer* hours of anyone I know.
4 Theresa has been much *happier/happy* since she got a promotion.
5 Steven's job is much *well/better* paid than mine.
6 Now that I've moved house I don't have as far to travel to work *as/than* I used to.

2 **Complete the second sentence so that it has a similar meaning to the first sentence. Use between three and five words.**

1 Megan's the best computer programmer in the department.
No one in the department is as .... Megan at computer programming.
2 I've never read such an impressive application letter.
This is .... application letter I've ever read.
3 Jean's not as experienced as Rob in managing people.
Jean .... than Rob in managing people.
4 The old machinery wasn't very good but the new machinery is very efficient.
The new machinery is .... the old machinery.
5 He's a very fair boss – more so than any other I've had.
He's a .... any other I've had.
6 I've never had such a bad job in my life.
This is .... I've ever had.

3 **Complete the dialogue with the comparative and superlative forms of the words in brackets.**

A: How are you enjoying your new job, Chris?
B: It's great, thanks. A lot of the people in my department are **(1)** .... (*old*) me and have worked for the company for a long time. They're **(2)** .... (*experienced*) me, which is good because I'm learning a lot from them. I'm starting to feel **(3)** .... (*confident*) in my role now.
A: That's good. Are your presentation skills improving too?
B: Yes! I gave my first presentation to new clients last week. It was **(4)** .... (*big*) group of people I've ever spoken to and it went really well.

Use of English

Open cloze ▶ CB page 63

1 Read the text in Activity 2 quickly. Is the writer talking about a part-time summer job or voluntary work experience?

2 Complete the text with the word which best fits each gap. Use only one word in each gap. There is an example at the beginning.

BLOG

I'm having the **(0)** *best* time in the Ecuadorian rainforest and I'm glad I decided to spend my gap year here before I go **(1)** .... university. I'm helping scientists protect the rainforest and the species of wildlife **(2)** .... live there. I work in a small team **(3)** .... other volunteers doing research and investigation work, collecting data and helping on construction projects. The first couple of weeks were tough **(4)** .... the climate and environment we're working in are very different from home. We **(5)** .... to do some training to help us understand the work and we also learned first aid and other skills, which helped us to feel safer. The days **(6)** .... long and tiring but it's really rewarding to think I'm doing something so worthwhile. We don't get paid but we get our accommodation and meals for free. I've learned loads **(7)** .... new stuff and the people I'm working with are cool. I'd love to come back **(8)** .... I've finished my studies!

Listening

Sentence completion ▶ CB page 64

1 ▶12 Look at the photo and the title. Then listen to the recording. Are statements 1 and 2 *true* (T) or *false* (F)?

1 The woman is a famous actress. ....
2 The woman works in the film industry. ....

2 ▶12 Listen again and complete each sentence with one word.

Zena Smith: My life as a stuntwoman

When Zena was a little girl, she particularly liked watching **(1)** .... films.

The first stunt people worked in **(2)** .... rather than action films.

Zena was encouraged to take part in a film by her **(3)** ....

Zena says that it is helpful to have skills such as skiing or **(4)** .... to get work as a stunt person.

Zena says it is not necessary to get what she calls a **(5)** '................' in stunt work.

Actors known as 'film extras' might do small parts, such as pretending to be **(6)** .... or just walking down a street.

When Zena was a stunt double for a famous actress, she was lucky to be the same **(7)** .... and body shape.

Zena was pleased when she won a small **(8)** .... for her stunt work.

Grammar

obligation and necessity ▶ CB page 65

1 Choose the correct option to complete the sentences.

1 I *don't have to/must* wear a uniform for my job. It's great because I can wear my jeans to work if I want to!

2 Peter *didn't have to/had to* leave home very early to get the train to work. He had a meeting at 7.00 a.m.!

3 We *were supposed to/had to* move to the new offices today but they still aren't ready.

4 You *mustn't/don't need to* switch the computers off – I'll do it before I leave.

5 You *are supposed to/should* ask for a pay rise. Your salary hasn't increased for three years.

6 You *need to/mustn't* handle food without washing your hands first because they could be dirty.

2 Complete the job advertisement with *must, have to, need to* or *don't have/need to*. Sometimes more than one form is possible.

MARKET RESEARCHER REQUIRED

This is a fantastic opportunity for the right person. Yummy Chocs Ltd require an in-store market researcher to collect customer feedback on samples of our premier chocolate ranges.

Here's what the role involves:
Placed in a variety of stores across the North West, you will meet customers on a daily basis, so you will **(1)** .... dress smartly at all times.

Talking to customers about their tastes is an essential part of this role, so you **(2)** .... be a friendly and sociable person.

You will be part of a team of co-workers who will get together regularly to discuss and analyse customer feedback. Therefore you **(3)** .... enjoy working with others to share your ideas.

You don't **(4)** .... have a qualification in food science or marketing but you **(5)** .... be passionate about chocolate.

You **(6)** .... send proof of qualifications at this point but if you think you've got what it takes, send your CV and covering letter to the address below.

Writing

Letter of application ▶ CB page 66

About the exam:
In the exam, you may have the option to write a letter of application.

Strategy:
• Make sure you include all the information asked for in the question.
• Write in an appropriate style.

1 Read the task and the candidate's letter. Which information has NOT been included?

You see this advertisement in a local newspaper.

Do you like working with children?
We're looking for an enthusiastic play worker for children at our holiday club. Applicants must be qualified and motivated.

Apply in writing, indicating your availability for interview to Mrs G. Randall at the address below.

Write your **letter of application**.

Hi, Mrs Randall,

I saw the job for a holiday club worker advertised in the newspaper last week and I want to apply for it. It looks very interesting.

I believe I could do the job very well. I am currently working as a nursery nurse and I really enjoy being with children. I am patient because I grew up in a family with a lot of children! I am enthusiastic and creative and I love thinking up new games for children to play. Regarding my formal training – I have qualifications in child care and I also speak three languages: French, Italian and German.

My job finishes at the end of June so I'll be free to work over the summer. If I get the job with you, I could start from 5th July. If you wish, I could send you references from two employers. I am attaching my CV with my contact details.

What's the pay and what are the hours?

Please write soon,
Yours faithfully,
Maria Benson
Maria Benson

2 Read the letter again and find four examples of language that is too informal.

3 Read another advertisement from the newspaper and write your letter of application. You should write between 140–190 words.

WANT TO WORK ON A FILM?

Over July and August, we shall be filming a new Robin Hood film in this area and we are looking for people to help with make-up and costume.

Apply to James Deacon at Weekes Films (address below) with details of your experience and availability.

Well-being

Speaking

Long turn ▶ CB page 70

1 Read the task and look at the photos below. Which of the comments 1–6 are relevant for Student A? Which comment is relevant for Student B?

Student A: Your pictures show people who are happy for different reasons. Compare the pictures and say why you think the people are happy.

Student B: What sort of music do you enjoy listening to most? Why?

---

1 He's probably listening to his favourite music.   ....
2 I would like to spend a holiday in this place.   ....
3 My favourite place to listen to music is in my bedroom.   ....
4 People are often happy when the weather is good.   ....
5 I really like rock music, especially Bryan Adams.   ....
6 The girl has probably said something funny.   ....

2 ▶ 13 Complete a candidate's answer with words from the box. Then listen and check.

Both   definitely   imagine   look   might   must   other
probably   seem   sure

I like these pictures! It's good to see people who are enjoying life. **(1)** .... the young guy with the iPod and the family **(2)** .... very happy. The guy has a contented smile on his face and the family are laughing. But the reasons they are happy are **(3)** .... quite different. I mean, the young guy is listening to music, he's alone but his eyes are closed so you can **(4)** .... that he's lost in his world of music. He **(5)** .... be in a park or relaxing in his back garden, but he's **(6)** .... away from all the stresses of life! The family, on the **(7)** .... hand, are in a busier place. They are probably on holiday and they **(8)** .... to be enjoying a meal outside together. For them and the boy, the weather looks good. I'm **(9)** .... the family are happy because they're together and relaxing and maybe someone has told a joke! It **(10)** .... be very enjoyable and exciting to eat a meal in a lovely place like that!

Use of English
Word formation ▶ CB page 71

1 **Add a prefix to make the opposites of adjectives 1–6.**

1 .... friendly
2 .... patient
3 .... loyal
4 .... responsible
5 .... lucky
6 .... complete

2 **Choose the correct alternative to complete the sentences.**

1 The pharmacist was very *helpful/helpless* and gave me some drops for my eyes.

2 That was a very *thoughtful/thoughtless* thing to say. I feel upset now.

3 Laughter is one of the most *powerless/powerful* medicines. It makes you feel better.

4 Don't worry about the dog! He's completely *harmful/harmless*.

5 The information the nurse gave me about asthma was very *useless/useful*. I know what to do now.

6 What a *colourful/colourless* room. I love orange!

3 **Read the article about what makes people happy. Use the word given in capitals at the end of the lines to form a word that fits in the gap in the same line.**

What *really* makes people happy?

According to **(0)** *psychologists*, what really makes people happy might, at first, seem rather **PSYCHOLOGY**
(1) .... Experts say that individual **EXPECT**
happiness levels are genetic, which is why some people manage to remain **(2)** .... even **HOPE**
when things are going wrong, whereas others find it **(3)** .... to lift themselves **POSSIBLE**
out of a bad mood. But it's not all in the mind: actions count too. A certain amount of life
(4) .... comes from spending time doing **SATISFY**
things we love. **(5)** .... which give us **ACTIVE**
'flow' – in other words, which keep us interested and focused, are **(6)** .... in **EFFECT**
helping us to forget our problems. Whether it's playing a **(7)** .... instrument or piloting **MUSIC**
a plane, the result is the same: doing things you're good at makes you feel better. Another thing that makes us feel happier is the
(8) .... to forgive others, as well as doing **ABLE**
things for people less fortunate than ourselves. So, let's get busy!

Vocabulary
health and fitness ▶ CB page 72

1 **Read the clues and complete the crossword.**

Across

1 You get this if you have an accident.
2 It's important to … fit if you want to stay healthy.
3 People are taken to hospital in this.
4 A way of hurting your ankle.
5 You can get a lot of this in red meat – like steak.

Down

1 If your body is in good … you won't have so many health problems.
2 This can help when you have a bad headache.
3 … exercise helps the heart stay strong.
4 This is the best type of diet to have.
5 A doctor will give you the right … for an illness.

2 **Complete the sentences with the correct form of words from the crossword.**

1 People who do a lot of exercise need a lot of .... in their diet.

2 I fell over during a football game and .... my ankle.

3 My aunt is over sixty but she's in good .... because she's always done a lot of exercise.

4 It isn't easy to .... fit if you're ill and in hospital.

5 My brother had a knee .... after a car accident and it took ages to get better.

6 For a .... diet you should eat a little bit of everything!

3 Choose the correct alternative to complete the sentences.

1 Apparently there are a lot of health *profits/benefits* to drinking tea.

2 I went *down/out* with flu after staying with my cousin last week.

3 I've got a new cream to rub onto *hurt/aching* muscles. It's great after football.

4 My mum makes sure that we all have a *balanced/fair* diet.

5 They say you can't *catch/take* a cold just from being in a low temperature.

6 How often do you work *up/out* in the gym?

7 Life *prediction/expectancy* is now something like 85 years for men.

8 I've got a *blocked/closed* nose and people can't understand what I'm saying!

9 I've *taken/picked* up a stomach bug and I really feel awful.

10 The doctor suggested taking cough *tablets/medicine* every four hours.

Grammar

zero, first and second conditionals
▶ CB page 73

1 Look at the internet forum about a new way of exercising. Complete the text with the correct form of the verbs in brackets.

2 Put the words in the correct order to make sentences or questions.

1 hungry, / eggs / fill me up / because / If / I'm / eat / I / they

....

2 would / twisted / you / ankle / do / if / your / What / you ?

....

3 take / I / painkiller / if / had / a / would / headache / a / I

....

4 you / information / I'll / you / that / give / it / want / if / diet

....

5 If / were / I / would / go / bed / earlier / you, / to / I

....

6 you / milk / muscles / exercise / after / ache / Do / if / drink / your ?

....

Tina123, 1/08/12, 8.14 a.m.

I watched this fascinating programme last night about exercise. It said that if you did just three minutes of intense exercise a week, you **(1)** .... (*get*) huge health benefits! Experts reckon that natural, everyday movement could be better for us than doing regular workout sessions at the gym. Apparently, doing quick bursts of exercise, where you run or cycle as hard as you can for less than a minute each time, keeps you fit. They said that if you exercise like this, it **(2)** .... (*keep*) you in shape, but it also makes you want to eat less – whereas exercising for longer periods makes you hungrier! Cool!

BusyBea, 01/08/12, 9.41 a.m.

I **(3)** .... (*be*) really annoyed if they find out this is true because I'm a personal trainer and my job depends on people employing me to help them do training workouts. I wouldn't get paid much if I only **(4)** .... (*work*) for three minutes with each customer!

Gino, 01/08/12, 2.03 p.m.

Well, I guess if you **(5)** .... (*be*) a lazy person, this way of exercising sounds like a great idea. But just three minutes of exercise a week?! That's ridiculous.

ZigZagZoo, 02/08/12, 1.31 a.m.

I work really long hours and don't have time to go to the gym. So, if this worked, I **(6)** .... (*find*) time to try it.

DanDan, 03/08/12, 6.15 p.m.

If you **(7)** .... (*not exercise*) you get fat and that's a fact. But only doing three minutes a week? Doesn't sound enough to me.

FunnyMouse, 03/08/12, 10.42 p.m.

Think of all the time you **(8)** .... (*save*) if this was true! Instead of being bored at the gym or jogging round the streets when it's dark in winter, you could be doing something much more interesting, like seeing friends or going to the cinema. Great idea!

Listening

Multiple matching ▶ CB page 74

1 ▶14 **Listen to four people talking about alternatives to seeing the doctor about health problems. Match speakers 1–4 with pictures A–D.**

A ....

B ....

C ....

D ....

2 ▶14 **Listen again and choose from the list A–E what each speaker does. There is one extra letter which you do not need to use.**

A uses information to decide whether to get professional help

B learns from strangers' experiences

C refers to advice given by a member of the family

D keeps up to date with modern advances in treatment

E enjoys learning about unfamiliar medical problems

Speaker 1 [ ]
Speaker 2 [ ]
Speaker 3 [ ]
Speaker 4 [ ]

Grammar

unless, otherwise, provided that
▶ CB page 75

1 **Find and correct the mistakes in the sentences. There is one mistake in each sentence.**

1 Provided that this cough clears up soon, I'll go to the doctor's for a prescription.

2 I must stop eating so much, provided that I'll get fat.

3 You'll have health problems otherwise you eat healthily and take regular exercise.

4 Steve wants to be a nurse unless he passes his final exams.

5 If you want, I'll give you a lift to the hospital. Unless I'll see you later instead.

6 Jenny said she would help me with my exercise plan this week unless she has the time.

2 **Complete the article with *unless, otherwise* or *provided that*.**

Vitamins and minerals

Toni Sherry asks whether we really need to take supplements

Open any health magazine and you'll see hundreds of adverts for vitamins and minerals. I've tried many of them, but I haven't noticed any real differences in my health. In fact, I think that **(1)** .... you have a particularly poor diet, you should get everything you need from what you eat. But am I right about this? I asked health expert Brian Peacock for advice.

'Yes, you're right,' he tells me. '**(2)** .... you stick to a healthy eating plan, you shouldn't need to take additional vitamins or minerals. **(3)** .... your body is suffering from a lack of a particular vitamin and your doctor gives you a prescription for something, you should be fine – **(4)** .... you could be taking more vitamins than your body actually needs.'

He goes on to tell me that beliefs have changed in the medical profession over the benefits of taking extra vitamins and minerals. '**(5)** .... you're pregnant, when taking folic acid is recommended, don't bother wasting your money. Buying vitamins from health food shops is expensive, so **(6)** .... you've been specifically advised to take them, leave them on the shelf.'

Reading

Multiple choice ▶ CB pages 76–77

1 Read the title of the magazine article. What kind of information do you think might be included in the text?

2 Now read the whole article. For questions 1–6, choose the answer (A, B or C) which you think fits best according to the text.

The world's craziest diets

Almost all of us want to lose a kilo or two or decide to at some time during our lives. But eating less and doing more exercise seem very sensible compared with some of the weird diets of the past few centuries. Here are some of the craziest.

The 'chewing diet' was invented by a man called Horace Fletcher and was popular during the early twentieth century. Fletcher believed that chewing allowed food to be properly absorbed into the body. To implement the chewing diet, a person must chew each bite over 32 times – which takes approximately 30 seconds per bite. It's a fascinating theory and there may appear to be some reason to this diet. I'm almost tempted to have a go – but surely it only works because it's so boring that you eat less!

If your food looks horrible, you're less likely to eat it. That's what people who believe in the 'vision diet' say, anyway. The idea is to wear blue glasses while you're eating so that your food looks disgusting. Why blue? Blue food doesn't occur often in the wild and plants that are blue are often poisonous – therefore food that's blue in colour doesn't look very inviting. Unsurprisingly, this diet doesn't really work and while some might enjoy the attention they receive while sitting in a restaurant wearing blue glasses, to do so for long periods could actually have a negative impact on your vision.

If you're showering every day, you might as well lose weight while doing it, right? Well, that's the theory behind Aoqili diet soaps. These special soaps contain seaweed that will get through your skin and break down fat. Does it work? While there may be evidence that seaweed breaks down fat when you eat it, there's no evidence for it working when washing and some people who've tried it have been allergic to the soaps, which made their skin itch. Isn't it their own fault for believing such a silly idea in the first place?

The 'cotton ball diet'. I'd say that this has to be one of the most dangerous diets for your body and it's difficult to understand how it ever became even slightly popular. The theory is that eating cotton balls – similar to the ones you clean your face with – prevents you wanting to eat anything fattening. This diet might be low in calories (which would usually keep the weight off) but it's not only dry and disgusting – it can also cause major damage to your body – which makes it very irresponsible to promote such a diet.

The theory behind the 'blood type diet' is that every blood type has a set of foods that are suited to it. Therefore, say supporters of this diet, if you eat according to your blood type, you'll lose weight. So, a person with type A blood should be vegetarian and a person with type O should avoid eating cereal or wheat, while type B can fill up on cream and yoghurts. This diet may seem harmless, but be careful – if you have an allergy to dairy foods, for example, doctors say you might be eating food that could cause your body serious problems.

Last but not least, we come to the 'caveman diet', which perhaps makes more sense than any of the other weird ideas. This diet is based on what cavemen ate 10,000 years ago, which means only eating food that could be hunted or picked locally – including meat, fish, vegetables, fruit and nuts. But, while *I* could probably manage without them, for some it must be difficult to avoid tasty things like bread, dairy products, salt, sugar or oils. The conclusion? This diet isn't dangerous and you can still eat out at restaurants on steak and salad, but you do need to make sure you're getting enough calcium – a mineral found in milk and cheese.

1 What does the writer say about the chewing diet?

A It seems to be a sensible diet to follow.

B She would like to try the diet.

C The diet doesn't take up much time to do.

2 The writer says that the vision diet

A attracts unwelcome looks from other diners.

B recreates something that is seen in nature.

C can cause sight problems for people who do it.

3 What suggestion does the writer make about the Aoqili soap diet?

A The diet requires considerable effort to do.

B The idea behind the diet is based on proof.

C The people who do it deserve the consequences.

4 What opinion does the writer express about the cotton ball diet?

A It is the least helpful for keeping weight down.

B It is wrong of people to suggest it is worth doing.

C It is a diet that stops you from feeling hungry.

5 When talking about the blood type diet, the writer uses the example of allergies to show that

A people should be cautious about trying the diet.

B doctors advise using this method of losing weight.

C people with type B blood suffer the most from the diet.

6 How does the writer feel about the caveman diet?

A She would not like to have to avoid all her favourite foods.

B She thinks it is a diet she would be able to stick to.

C She is glad that restaurants provide options for caveman dieters.

3 Complete the sentences with the prepositions in the box.

from   in   on   to (x4)   with

1 I'm tempted _____ eat some of that chocolate cake but I know I shouldn't.

2 Jed doesn't eat prawns because he's allergic _____ them.

3 You should eat a healthy diet based _____ fresh vegetables, white meat and fruit.

4 Eating plenty of green, leafy vegetables can prevent you _____ getting cancer.

5 Vitamins occur _____ fresh, unprocessed foods.

6 Too much fat in your diet can cause damage _____ your heart.

7 Compared _____ some other food types, there is a lot of iron in red meat.

8 According _____ my doctor, I should cut down on the number of eggs I eat.

Writing

Informal email ▶ CB page 79

1 Read the exam task. Underline the phrases in the email extract that show it is written in an informal style.

You have received an email from your Canadian friend, Pam. Read this part of the email and then write your **email** to Pam.

I've got end of year exams next week and I'm having real problems revising! There seems so much to do and I can't concentrate! Help! Any ideas?

Love,

Pam

2 Here are some sentences from the reply. Which sentences are NOT relevant?

1 I'm not good at revising, either.

2 How did the exams go?

3 Make sure you take lots of breaks.

4 It's a good idea to plan a revision schedule.

5 Forget about it. Enjoy yourself!

6 It sometimes helps to work with a friend.

7 If you want me to check your work, that's not a problem.

8 I find that I concentrate best in the evenings.

3 Complete phrases 1–6 with the words in the box. Then write your email, including all the phrases. Write 140–190 words.

about   don't   hear   idea   sorry   well

1 It's good to _____ that …

2 I'm _____ to hear that.

3 Hope all goes _____!

4 That sounds a great _____.

5 Why _____ you … ?

6 Or how _____ … ?

Nature study

8

Vocabulary

animals ▶ CB page 80

1 **Choose one word in each group that does NOT fit.**

1	reptile	insect	cat	mammal
2	feathers	wings	fur	scales
3	fins	paws	claws	fish
4	bear	crocodile	salmon	shark
5	dragonfly	owl	snake	kingfisher

2 **Decide if statements 1–10 are *true* (T) or *false* (F).**

1 Fish use their fins to breathe. ....
2 Kingfishers live in the water. ....
3 Bears have brown skin. ....
4 Owls usually hunt at night. ....
5 Dragonflies use their paws to fly. ....
6 Salmon eat with their beaks. ....
7 Snakes don't have claws. ....
8 Reptiles can swim, crawl and fly. ....
9 Ants live in large groups. ....
10 Crocodiles are covered in fur. ....

Listening

Multiple choice ▶ CB page 81

1 ▶ 15 **Listen to part of a radio interview and answer the questions.**

1 Who is Michelle? ....
2 Who is Rufus? ....

2 ▶ 15 Listen again. For questions 1–6, choose the best answer (A, B or C).

1 How did Michelle feel before she got her guide dog, Rufus?

  A worried that he might get bored

  B relieved that he behaved so well

  C surprised by how intelligent he was

2 What did Michelle find most difficult about training with Rufus?

  A learning to look after him properly

  B memorising what instructions to give him

  C remembering to give him time to run around

3 What is the biggest change that Michelle has experienced since having a guide dog?

  A becoming more independent

  B having more friends

  C being less scared

4 Why did the guide dog trainers choose Rufus for Michelle?

  A He likes to be active.

  B He's a small animal.

  C He likes to walk quickly.

5 What does Michelle say about taking Rufus to college?

  A She lets her friends play with him.

  B He enjoys the attention he gets.

  C He cannot be with her at certain times.

6 What does Michelle like most about Rufus?

  A He can be very funny.

  B He makes her feel better.

  C He gets on well with her family.

3 ▶ 15 Listen again and write M (Michelle) or R (Rufus) for each description.

1 independent ....

2 friendly ....

3 intelligent ....

4 active ....

5 has a great sense of humour ....

6 tall ....

Grammar

passive forms   ▶ CB page 82

1 Complete the sentences with the passive form of the verbs in brackets.

1 Zoo animals .... (*look after*) very well these days.

2 My dog Zack .... (*see*) by the vet at the moment.

3 The kitten .... (*rescue*) by the fire service when he got stuck up a tree.

4 The fences .... (*repair*) at the safari park because a small animal escaped!

5 I've just had a call from the stables to say my horse .... (*steal*)! I can't believe that's happened.

6 The animal rescue centre .... (*give*) a large donation by the local government.

2 Complete the text with the active or passive form of the verbs in brackets.

RUDYARD KIPLING'S JUST SO STORIES

Rudyard Kipling was a British author who wrote a series of stories for children called the *Just So Stories*. These fabulous tales are a work of fantasy, in which strange things happen to animals and people. They **(1)** .... (*first publish*) in 1902 and they describe how animals – in the writer's imagination – **(2)** .... (*change*) from their original form to how they appear today. Some changes **(3)** .... (*make*) by humans, while others happened magically.

In *How the Camel got his Hump*, the camel **(4)** .... (*give*) the hump on his back as a punishment for refusing to work, and in *The Sing-song of Old Man Kangaroo*, we find out how the kangaroo got his powerful back legs from **(5)** .... (*chase*) by a wild dog all day. The dog **(6)** .... (*send*) to chase the kangaroo, after the kangaroo **(7)** .... (*ask*) to be made different from all other animals. The original editions of the stories **(8)** .... (*illustrate*) by the author himself and they **(9)** .... (*still enjoy*) by children and adults today. Editions of the stories **(10)** .... (*also release*) on DVD, so that people can watch them too.

Speaking
Collaborative task ▶ CB page 83

1 ▶ 16 **Listen to the examiner's instructions and complete the task.**

Here are some things **(1)** _____ can do to help the environment. Talk to each other about **(2)** _____ these things can help the environment. Now you have a minute to decide which is the most **(3)** _____ .

2 ▶ 17 **Complete the extract from the conversation with the words in the box. Then listen and check.**

again	know	mean (x2)	right	say
saying	understand			

A: So, we have to **(1)** _____ how these things can help the environment. Is that **(2)** _____ ?

B: OK, well, obviously recycling your rubbish is really important. It helps because then we don't put so much stuff into landfill sites.

A: What do you **(3)** _____ , 'landfill'?

B: That's what they call those great big rubbish dumps in the countryside. You **(4)** _____ , the rubbish stays there for ages.

A: OK. Yeah – we reuse things and don't have to use energy and new materials to make things from scratch.

B: You **(5)** _____ – like clothes and things?

A: Exactly. What about the food for birds? Do you think that's very helpful?

B: Well, yes. Because with climate change a lot of bird species are dying out.

A: Sorry, I don't **(6)** _____ .

B: Sometimes the winters are harder and they can't find food, or the summers are hotter and they don't get enough water.

A: So, are you **(7)** _____ that it's more important to feed birds than recycle rubbish?

B: No, I'm just pointing out that a lot of our wildlife is having a bad time and it's good to help, don't you agree?

A: Could you say that **(8)** _____ ?

B: It's good to help …

A: Sorry, I meant the bit about the wildlife.

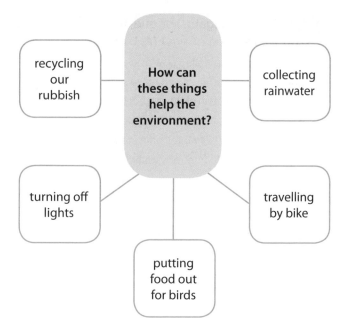

3 **Match questions 1–5 with the candidate's answers A–E.**

1 Do you do any of these things or know someone who does? _____

2 Do you think governments should do more to help the environment? _____

3 Is the climate in your country changing a lot? How? _____

4 Should schools teach children about the environment when they are very young? Why/Why not? _____

5 Do you think it's too late for us to do anything about environmental problems? Why/Why not? _____

A Actually it is. We get a lot more rain than we used to. Also, we've had some very cold winters recently.

B No. There's a lot we can do. The problem is that people don't like changing their habits!

C A friend of mine has bought an electric car but at the moment there aren't many places he can charge it! So, he can't travel very far.

D Definitely. Because people like you and me can't do a lot. There need to be big changes.

E I think so. In my country they do. And also even before they start. My young sister had some books about things like recycling before she started school!

Reading

Gapped text ▶ CB pages 84–85

1 Read an article about a famous conservationist who adopted a herd of elephants. What did he learn from the elephants?

2 Read the article again. Six sentences have been removed from the article. You have to choose from sentences A–G the one which best fits each gap. There is one extra sentence which you do not need to use.

A A few years later, when Anthony's first grandchild, Ethan, was born, he did the same.

B And not just a normal herd of elephants, but a notorious, wild herd that had caused damage to huge areas of KwaZulu-Natal in South Africa.

C But also, he had no idea that a group of troublesome elephants would teach him a lot about family love and loyalty.

D In spite of this, the young elephants treat the older ones with respect and love.

E And one morning, instead of trying to get out, she just stood there.

F Every morning, the elephants would try to break out of the compound where they were living.

G Angry elephants can be very dangerous animals if they don't like you.

3 Complete the sentences with the underlined words in the article.

1 The animals have a _____ life when there is no rain for months.

2 Someone _____ the glass in the window to break into our house.

3 When my dad got a job on the nature magazine it was a _____ in his career.

4 It's important for children to _____ their teachers.

5 The survey produced some _____ results that no one had predicted.

6 I'll _____ my parents to let me go on holiday to Africa with my best friend.

THE HERD INSTINCT

Ten years ago, the conservationist Lawrence Anthony adopted seven wild elephants in South Africa.

Lawrence Anthony remembers the moment he met his ready-made family for the first time. 'They were a difficult group, no question about it,' he says. 'Very naughty. But I could see a lot of good in them too. They'd had a <u>tough</u> time and were all scared and yet they were looking after one another, trying to protect one another.'

From the way he talks, you might think that he was talking about problem children; in fact, it's a herd of elephants. **1** Farmers were now threatening to shoot them. 'I was their only hope,' says Anthony, 59. 'There were seven of them in all, including babies and a teenage son. But the previous owner had had enough of them – they'd <u>smashed</u> their way through every fence he had.'

Anthony knew dealing with elephants like this was risky. **2** But when an elephant-welfare organisation spoke to them, Anthony, a respected conservationist, knew he couldn't refuse.

Today he says that he had never imagined the job would be so hard. 'It's been a hundred times harder than I'd thought,' he says. **3** 'The care these elephants have for each other is <u>astounding</u>,' he says. From the start, Anthony considered the elephants part of his family. 'We called the oldest mother Nana, because that's what all the children in the Anthony family call my mum,' he says.

As with human adoptions, the early days were especially difficult. **4** Every day, Anthony, like many parents who have to deal with difficult kids, would try to persuade them not to behave badly. 'I'd go down to the fence and I'd <u>beg</u> Nana not to break it down,' he says. 'I knew she didn't understand English, but I hoped she'd understand by the tone of my voice and my body language what I was saying. **5** Then she put her trunk through the fence towards me. I knew she wanted to touch me – elephants are tremendously tactile, they use touch all the time to show concern and love. That was a <u>turning point</u>.'

Today, the Anthonys are so close to their elephants that occasionally they have almost had to chase them out of the sitting room! Anthony has always believed that if he respected them, they would <u>respect</u> him. When Nana's son, Mvula was born, she brought the baby to Anthony. She wanted to show him to the man who she now considered part of her family. **6** 'Mind you,' he says with a laugh, 'my daughter-in-law didn't talk to me for a long time afterwards. There I was, holding her tiny baby, walking towards a herd of wild elephants. The elephants were so excited – their trunks went straight up and they all came closer, completely focused on the little child in my arms, sniffing the air to get the smell. I was trusting them with my baby, just as they had trusted me with theirs.'

Adopting a herd of wild elephants was probably the biggest risk Anthony ever took, but it worked. He is now as much a part of their family as they are of his.

Grammar

causative *have* ▶ CB page 86

1 Complete the second sentence so that it has a similar meaning to the first. Use the causative *have*.

Example: We built a new shed for our garden tools.
We had a new shed built for our garden tools.

1 We have made our garden into a habitat for butterflies.
We .... into a habitat for butterflies.

2 We've replaced our old windows with double glazing.
We .... with double glazing.

3 We installed a solar panel on our roof.
We .... on our roof.

4 We fitted some curtains that keep in the heat.
We .... that keep in the heat.

5 We're going to make some of our lawn into a vegetable patch.
We .... into a vegetable patch.

6 We replaced our coal fire with a wood burner.
We .... with a wood burner.

Use of English

key word transformations ▶ CB page 87

1 Complete the sentences with the prepositions in the box.

| about | after | for | of (x3) | on | with |

1 I think it's important to look .... our local environment for the people who live here.

2 Poor little dog! He's in desperate need .... a drink after that long walk in the heat.

3 We should take advantage .... new energy-saving devices.

4 Local residents are .... bad terms with the council for not collecting their rubbish.

5 Ted is passionate .... making his town a greener place.

6 Climate change isn't going to be good .... many animals.

7 Oh! I can't use the snack machine – it's out .... order.

8 There's no point in getting annoyed .... me. There's nothing I can do to change things!

2 For sentences 1–6, complete the second sentence so that it has a similar meaning to the first sentence, using the word given. Do not change the word given. You must use between two and five words including the word given.

Example: The town council have decided they need to provide more recycling bins.
BE
The town council have decided that more recycling bins *need to be provided* .

1 Terry washed his car at the carwash.
HAD
Terry .... at the carwash.

2 I didn't mean to break the window – it was an accident.
PURPOSE
I broke the window by accident – I didn't ....

3 The hurricane caused a lot of damage to buildings around the city.
BY
A lot of damage .... to buildings around the city.

4 Rainwater has collected in a tub in my garden. It's completely full.
UP
Rainwater .... a tub in my garden.

5 I've noticed changes in the weather over the last few years.
BEEN
There .... in the weather over the last few years.

6 I'm not sure about the idea of keeping a pet dog in a busy town.
WHETHER
I don't know .... good idea to keep a pet dog in a busy town.

7 It is necessary to find new ways to reduce our energy usage.
NEED
We .... new ways to reduce our energy usage.

8 We can reduce air pollution in cities by changing to electric cars.
BE
Air pollution in cities .... by changing to electric cars.

Writing

Article ▶ CB page 88

1 Read the exam task and the article. Which points do you think the writer would be wrong to include?

> You have seen the following notice in an international nature magazine.
>
> ### Animals in danger!
>
> Write an article about an endangered animal in your area or country, saying why it is endangered. We shall publish the best three in next month's magazine.
>
> Write your article in **140–190** words.

1 whether it's good to keep these animals in captivity
2 how many animals there are left
3 a detailed description of a campaign to save the animal
4 reasons for the animal's problems
5 their own opinion about the situation

2 Read the article again and answer the questions.

1 Which animal is mentioned?
2 Why is it endangered?
3 What is the writer's opinion?

SADLY MISSED!

There's an animal that I really love and sadly it is quickly disappearing from our area. This is a very pretty and clever animal that we used to see all over the UK. Now we can only see it in a few protected places, such as the Isle of Wight and some parts of Scotland. This animal is the red squirrel.

So, why is this beautiful animal disappearing? Are humans destroying its habitats? Are we hunting it for food? Or is it perhaps because of the changing climate? The answer to all these questions is no! Red Squirrels are dying out because of a clever invader.

Grey squirrels, not native to the UK, somehow crossed the Atlantic from northern American in the nineteenth century. Because they are bigger and stronger than the reds, they take all the food and the red squirrels can't survive in the same area. The greys are pushing them out!

This is a real shame. Unfortunately, we are losing many animal and plant species because of unwanted invaders from other parts of the world. Perhaps people should not be the only ones to have passports and security checks when they enter the country!

3 Find these words in the article that show the writer's use of a range of vocabulary.

1 two adverbs that show the writer's opinion ....
2 four adjectives to describe the red squirrels ....
3 four adjectives to describe the grey squirrels ....
4 two phrasal verbs ....
5 a verb that means 'manage to live' ....
6 a verb that means 'chase' ....
7 a noun that means 'place where an animal lives' ....
8 a noun that means 'uninvited visitor' ....

4 Are these alternatives for parts of the article better than those used by the writer?

1 Title: The Red Squirrel
2 Opening sentence: The red squirrel is a beautiful animal which cannot be seen very often in our area today.
3 Opening – second paragraph: The red squirrel is not in danger because of climate change or because humans are destroying its habitat.
4 Opening – final paragraph: In my opinion, the red squirrel will be missed.

5 Read the exam task again. Make notes and write your own article in 140–190 words.

Future society

9

Listening

Sentence completion ▶ CB page 90

1 ▶ 18 **Listen to Lottie talking about the design of future homes and answer the questions.**

1 Who is she talking to? ....

2 What has she done? ....

2 ▶ 18 **Listen again. For questions 1–10, complete the sentences.**

1 According to Lottie, the building materials of the future will cope with difficult .... conditions.

2 Lottie thinks that each home will eventually be equipped with a .... machine to deal with waste.

3 Lottie says supermarkets will become more conscious of the quantity of .... they use.

4 Lottie has designed a .... which will reduce the amount of laundry that needs to be done.

5 Lottie is currently designing a new kind of .... that will clean itself.

6 A device that recognises .... will solve problems of household security.

7 Lottie is particularly proud of a piece of equipment that contains a .... that she has designed.

8 Lottie believes we'll avoid making meals by choosing a .... and instructing a special pot to cook it for us.

9 When our food supplies are running out, Lottie says our .... will be able to place orders for more.

10 Wearing a special .... will help family members to relax at home.

Vocabulary

computers ▶ CB page 91

1 **Choose the correct alternative to complete the sentences.**

1 I bought a second *printer/monitor* so that I could use two screens while I'm working.

2 The letter E is the one that is used most often on people's *screens/keyboards*.

3 It took a long time to install the new *software/passwords* on my computer.

4 My *application/avatar* in the role play game is tall with dark hair and is very athletic.

5 I know I shouldn't but I have to write down my *passwords/titles* or I forget them.

6 I *enclosed/attached* the file to my email but for some reason it didn't arrive.

2 **Complete the sentences from a computer manual with the correct form of the verbs in the box.**

bring	Click	crash	Download	enter	Log
lose	print	save	Scroll		

MANUAL

1 You must .... the changes to your document or you'll .... all your new work.

2 .... on 'file' and .... up the menu.

3 .... down the list of websites and find the most useful one.

4 .... onto your computer by .... a password.

5 .... the information from the internet and then you can .... it out.

6 If your computer ...., you can sometimes recover data from the hard drive.

Grammar

future perfect and continuous
▶ CB page 92

1 **Choose the correct alternative to complete the sentences.**

1 There's no way we'*ll be living/'ll have lived* on the moon any time soon.

2 I'm so pleased John *will be making/will have made* dinner by the time I get home. He said it will be on the table waiting, so I won't have to cook.

3 At this time tomorrow I'*ll be swimming/'ll have swum* in the hotel pool. It'll be great!

4 I'm going to make sure my son *will be learning/will have learned* the alphabet by the time he goes to school. He'll know all the letters.

5 I'm in so much debt I'*ll be paying it off/'ll have paid it off* 'til I'm sixty!

6 I hope we'*ll all be using/'ll all have used* renewable energy regularly by the time our natural resources run out.

7 David *will be going/will have gone* to the tennis club when he finishes his homework.

8 The council *will be spending/will have spent* its entire budget by the end of summer. They'll have nothing left.

2 **Complete the dialogue with the future perfect or continuous form of the verbs in brackets.**

Rob: What do you think you **(1)** .... (*do*) this time next year, Gina?

Gina: Well, by then I **(2)** .... (*finish*) my final exams, so I think I **(3)** .... (*celebrate*)! I **(4)** .... (*enjoy*) my holiday and I **(5)** .... (*sunbathe*) on a beach somewhere hot. What about you, Rob?

Rob: Well, I've just finished my own studies, so I hope by next June I **(6)** .... (*find*) a decent job. If I'm lucky, I **(7)** .... (*earn*) lots of money and I **(8)** .... (*buy*) myself a car!

Gina: Fingers crossed, then!

Speaking

Long turn ▶ CB page 93

1 **Look at the pictures and some comments students made. Complete their phrases with the words in the box.**

call	exact	gone	remember	thing

1 He's wearing a ..., what do you .... it? When the jacket and trousers are the same.

2 He's standing on the ..., I can't remember the .... word. It's where you wait for a train.

3 One boy is checking some notes in a ..., sorry, I don't .... the word.

4 It's the .... you keep papers and notes in at school.

5 The businessman has got a ..., sorry, it's ....

2 **Match the words A–D with comments 1–4 in Activity 1.**

A folder ....   C suit ....

B platform ....   D briefcase ....

3 **Read the task and two students' answers. Match comments 1–4 with answers A or B. Which do you think is the better answer?**

1 This answer describes the pictures only. ....

2 This answer says why the people are travelling. ....

3 This answer says why the people are using laptops. ....

4 This answer compares the pictures. ....

> Your pictures show people using laptops while travelling. Compare the pictures and say why you think the people are using the laptops while they are travelling.

A: The man in the first picture is at a station. He's waiting for a train. It's quite a nice day – at least, it isn't raining! In the background I can see a train which is coming to the station. He's soon going to get on it. I think he looks like a businessman because he's wearing a suit and he's got a briefcase. He probably prefers to travel by train because it's better than sitting in a traffic jam in his car. In the second picture, the two boys are already on the train. They're probably going to school or college or maybe they're coming home. I think it's summer because one boy is wearing a T-shirt and he's got sunglasses. I think they like travelling on the train. They probably do it every day. They can do their homework together.

B: All the people in the pictures are travelling. The man on the platform is waiting for a train whereas the boys are already on the train and probably travelling to school. The man at the station looks like a businessman – he's got a black briefcase – and he's using his laptop while he's waiting. I imagine that he has a lot of work to do and he can't waste a minute. He might be contacting his clients, or he could be reading his emails and planning his day. The boys, on the other hand, are probably working together to do some homework, or perhaps prepare for a test. None of the people look very stressed so I think this is part of their normal routine and they haven't got a big problem. It's good to travel by train because then you can use your laptop to catch up on things.

4 **Which do you think is the best follow-up question for this task?**

1 Do you like wearing a suit? ☐

2 Do you enjoy travelling by train? ☐

3 Do you often use a laptop while you're travelling? ☐

Reading
Multiple choice ▶ CB pages 94–95

1 **Read the questions and text about films that predicted the future. Underline the part of the text where you think the answer is.**

1 In the first paragraph of the text, the writer says that

A films that are made today reflect modern society.

B science fiction films weren't very good in the past.

C he thinks old sci-fi films are amusing to watch.

D some old films guessed the future correctly.

2 When talking about *Forbidden Planet*, the writer makes the point that

A the characters in the film were the first to use modern mobiles.

B it is unfortunate that the film's predictions didn't come true.

C the film made predictions that didn't come true for a long time.

D the film helped to bring about the progress of technology.

3 What does the writer say when talking about *The Truman Show*?

A It was unlike any other film that had been made about reality TV.

B Its main character was unaware of the role he was playing.

C People are more interested in celebrities then they should be.

D People who take part in reality TV shows are keen to become famous.

4 What does *observes* mean in line 58?

A wants   B notices   C cares   D ignores

5 When talking about *Minority Report*, the writer says that

A we are already experiencing similar technology to that seen in the film.

B the main character is confused by what he sees in the shopping centre.

C it is likely that all the film's predictions will eventually come true.

D he doesn't like being exploited by advertising companies.

6 In the final paragraph, the writer expresses the opinion that

A we are all worried about what will happen in the future.

B we are unlikely to do certain things that have been suggested.

C we will continue to see inventive ideas in films.

D we are eager to believe the fantasies we are sold in films.

2 Read the article again and answer the questions in Activity 1. For questions 1–6, choose the answer (A, B, C or D) which you think fits best according to the text.

Films that predicted the future

As humans we are obsessed with the future and this is reflected in films which predict what future society and technology will be like. It's easy enough to laugh at old sci-fi films but many contained details which proved to be an accurate prediction of life to come. Let's take a quick look at one or two from the last few decades.

Forbidden Planet, a science fiction film released in 1956, was the first film that was set in space and was one of the first of the modern sci-fi films that predicted life in the future. The film's characters were shown using handheld 'communicators' that they would carry everywhere with them, much like we do with our mobile phones today. This was one prediction that came well ahead of its time – it took another forty years before the use of mobile phones became widespread.

In 1998, when *The Truman Show* was released, there were very few TV reality shows around. This film follows the life of insurance salesman, Truman Burbank, who does not at first realise that he is the focus of a reality TV show which is broadcast to millions of people around the world. These days, TV is full of such shows, and while – unlike Truman – the people involved agree to take part in them, the shows reflect society's current fascination with celebrity.

It might have been an interesting idea to make a film about someone's day-to-day life in 1998, but these days we can't turn on the TV without seeing yet another weird and wonderful version of reality on shows like *Big Brother* or *Real Housewives*. Audiences, it seems, just can't get enough of them. It seems they are here to stay – for the foreseeable future, at least.

Another sci-fi film, this time a bit more recent, is *Minority Report*, which came out in 2002. While most of the film's predictions haven't come true (yet), in one scene of this popular film, the main character is seen walking through a shopping mall where his eyes are scanned by 3D screens. As he looks around him, he **observes** that the adverts he sees on the screens are directly aimed at him – screens even call his name to attract his attention, which they eventually get. It's certainly a strange scene but are we already halfway there? Think about when you use the internet to search for something. If you often look up books, for example, you'll soon start seeing adverts pop up on your screen for new titles because your computer saves your searches. The film was actually set in 2054, so perhaps by then some of the film's other predictions, like crimes being prevented before they happen, might have come true.

Have we seen it all now? I doubt it. Interested as we are in technological advances and our own personal futures, I'm sure there is plenty yet to come from the imaginative minds of sci-fi scriptwriters. And perhaps living on the moon isn't as far away as we think.

58

Grammar
reported speech ▶ CB page 96

1 **Change the sentences into reported speech.**

1 'As humans we are obsessed with the future,' says sci-fi director, Ken Smithies.

....

2 'It took forty years before the use of mobile phones became widespread,' he said.

....

3 'TV reality shows reflect society's fascination with celebrity,' said the reporter.

....

4 'Most of the film's predictions haven't come true yet,' reports Ken.

....

5 'Do we really want to mess with our minds?' the scientist asked.

....

6 'I'm sure there is still plenty to come from the imaginations of scriptwriters,' she told me.

....

2 **Read the text about students' hopes for the future and complete the text below using reported speech.**

Meg said that she **(1)** .... (do) a survey about what students at her school hoped to do in the future. She said she **(2)** .... (interview) fifty people so far. This is what a few of them said: Judie, who's 14, said she **(3)** .... (take) ballet classes since she was five but she had grown too tall to become a professional dancer. She said she **(4)** .... (be) a teacher instead. Michel said he had been asked to sign for a professional youth team and that he **(5)** .... (start) training soon. Sonia said she **(6)** .... (not know) what she wanted to do, but she said she might become a scientist. Jared said he **(7)** .... (be) really into rock climbing and he hoped to climb the highest mountains in the world. Linda said she **(8)** .... (go) on a trip to an airport and thought being an air traffic controller would be exciting. Meg said that she would put the full survey on the school website and she told us to take a look.

I'm doing a survey about what students at my school hope to do in the future. So far, I've interviewed fifty people. Here's what a few of them said:

Judie, 14: 'Well, I've been taking ballet classes since I was five and I always wanted to be a professional dancer. The problem is I've grown too tall to become a ballet dancer, so I'm going to teach it instead.'

Michel, 15: 'I'm going to be a footballer! I've already been asked to sign for a professional youth team and I'll start training soon!'

Sonia, 13: 'I don't know what I want to do yet. I like maths and science, so I might become a scientist.'

Jared, 16: 'I'm really into rock climbing outside of school, so I hope to climb all the highest mountains in the world!'

Linda, 11: 'I've just been on a school trip to an airport and I'd love to be an air traffic controller – how exciting would that be?!'

I'll put my full survey on the school website next week – don't forget to take a look!

Megan

3 **Report these comments from three more students.**

Jacky: I'm planning to take my school exams and then go to college for three years. I'd really like to study Art History.

Jim: I've always wanted to be an actor! I'll probably go to drama school for a couple of years and then audition for parts on television.

Simon: My dream is to be a racing driver – in Formula 1, like Lewis Hamilton! I've been doing a lot of karting recently and I've won a lot of prizes, so maybe one day my dream will come true!

1 ....

2 ....

3 ....

Use of English
Open cloze ▶ CB page 97

1 You are going to read an article about the future of food. Scan the text. Which foods in the box are mentioned?

cheese   insects   meat   rice   seaweed   vegetables

2 Read the article again and think of the word which best fits each gap.

THE FUTURE OF FOOD

In another few years, the world's population will **(0)** _have_ almost doubled. The question is, **(1)** _____ are we going to feed everyone? Scientists have come up **(2)** _____ several bright ideas. Here are a few of **(3)** _____ .

The first idea is artificial meat. Scientists believe they will be able to 'grow' meat from stem cells. It will look and taste exactly the same, even **(4)** _____ it hasn't come from an animal. The second idea is eating insects. Rich **(5)** _____ protein, vitamins and fats, these are already eaten in many countries around the world. With food prices increasing and a lack **(6)** _____ available land, it's possible **(7)** _____ before too long, insect farming will have become popular. And last but not least, super rice. This is a variety of rice that has already **(8)** _____ developed in China. Not only does it produce lots of grain, but it is also resistant to drought, floods and disease.

Writing
Report ▶ CB page 98

1 Read the exam task and the report. Complete the report with the words in the box.

aim   although   appears   expected
number   percent   said   worth

After a class discussion about how much people use computers these days, you have done a survey in your school about what students use their computers for.

Write a **report** for the school magazine about your results.

Introduction

The **(1)** _____ of this report is to show how the students at Barton College use their computers.

Research

A large **(2)** _____ of the students go online to do research for their homework and special projects. Most students **(3)** _____ that they spend several hours a day on their computers for this reason.

Communication

Again, most students use email or skype every day to contact their friends or family and about a third of students said that they use chat rooms at least twice a week, **(4)** _____ this is usually at weekends.

Games

Fewer students than **(5)** _____ play computer games regularly. A small number play for an hour or more every day. About fifty **(6)** _____ seem to play for a few hours at the weekends. Just one or two students said that this was their main use of the computer.

Conclusion

It **(7)** _____ from the results that computers are mainly used for study-related activities, with short but regular time spent on communicating. It may be **(8)** _____ carrying out another survey during holiday time to compare the results.

2 Match phrases 1–6 with the underlined phrases in the report.

1 It might be useful to _____
2 This report has been written to _____
3 The results seem to show _____
4 Lots of _____
5 According to the majority of students _____
6 An unexpected number of students _____

3 Read the exam task below and write your report.

You have done a survey of the students in your college to find out what students use their mobile phones for. Write a **report** for the college magazine about your results.

Write your report in **140–190** words.

Global Culture

10

Reading

Multiple matching ▶ CB pages 102–103

1 Read a magazine article about people's favourite performances quickly and decide if the statements are *true* (T) or *false* (F).

1 All the people went to theatrical performances. ....

2 Their favourite performers were all male. ....

2 Read the article again and for questions 1–10, choose from people A–D. The people may be chosen more than once.

Which person

had not expected to enjoy the performance? `1` ☐

watched a performance of something made famous by another person? `2` ☐

knew exactly what to expect in the performance? ☐

prefers theatre to cinema? `4` ☐

watched a performance of fictional events? `5` ☐

was reminded of a family member? `6` ☐

appreciates more than one form of entertainment? `7` ☐

enjoys the preparations before going to see a show? `8` ☐

has a different opinion to many others about a particular form of entertainment? `9` ☐

found a large part of the performance amusing? `10` ☐

3 Complete the sentences with the correct form of verbs from the article.

1 At the end of the show, I .... so hard that my hands hurt!

2 I couldn't .... my eyes off the main actor. He was incredible.

3 I wouldn't advise anyone to .... through that film. It was terrible.

4 Everyone .... loudly when the singer won the prize.

5 It's nice to .... dressed up to go to a party or a show.

6 The actor only played a small part but he later .... on to become a famous film star in Hollywood.

A memorable performance!

We asked four readers about the best performances they've seen.

A Donna

I love going out to the theatre and I enjoy all types of shows, from comedy to musicals and dramas. It's the whole thing, getting dressed up and looking forward to it. Also, it's brilliant being part of an audience. You can feel the atmosphere and see how different people react to what's on the stage. Live performances are so much better than film or TV for me. I think one of the best performances I've ever seen was during a play called *Shadowlands*. The play is about C S Lewis, the man who wrote the Narnia books – you know, *The Lion, the Witch and the Wardrobe*? He fell in love with an American poet called Joy Gresham but she died quite young and he was heart-broken. Both the main characters were wonderful but the actress playing Joy was superb.

B Martin

I was only a teenager – about fourteen, I think – when I went with the family to see the musical, *Les Miserables* in London. It's set at a particular time in France but the story is imaginary. The show was part of a day trip and we'd spent the morning going round the sights, so we were pretty tired by mid-afternoon, which is when we saw the performance. It was a matinee but the theatre was completely full. I wasn't particularly into the theatre at that time! But that performance really changed my opinion. It was magnificent. From the opening moments of the show to the final song – I couldn't take my eyes off the stage. I've been back to see it again and again since then. I was particularly impressed by the male singer who was the lead, Jean Valjean – his voice was amazingly powerful. And at the end everyone stood up and clapped and cheered for ages.

C Kelly

A lot of people think that talent shows on the TV don't really produce good singers but I definitely don't agree. I always choose my favourite and then I vote for them every Saturday! A couple of years back, my favourite was a young male singer called Matt Cardle. I remember he wore a hat and looked a bit like my cousin, Billy. I thought he had a great voice. He went on to win the TV show, which was great. Then, for a surprise Christmas present, my mum paid for me and my best friend to go to see the singers from the show when they went on tour. Matt sang 'The first time ever I saw your face', a song that Roberta Flack had sung a long time ago and I cried. I'll never forget how much it moved me.

D Mary

It sounds odd but one of the most memorable performances I've seen wasn't by a person but a dog! It was a film made from a book I had read, called *Marley and Me*. It was a real story about a journalist who gets a dog that is really badly behaved. Most of the book is very funny but the ending is really sad. When they made the film, I knew I had to see it but I was a bit worried about how I'd feel at the end. Well – the film was good, mostly very funny with some clever dog acting but at the end the dog playing Marley was perfect. I'm not a very sensitive person and I don't normally cry at the end of sad films but I did with this one! I don't believe anyone could sit through that film and NOT cry. It's impossible.

Grammar

relative pronouns and relative clauses
▶ CB page 104

1 **Complete the sentences with *who, which, that, where, when* or *whose*.**

1 That's the woman .... asked me for directions. She's lost.

2 She's the girl .... dog ran into our garden.

3 This is the map .... will show you where your hotel is.

4 I suppose I could see you at seven but that's the time .... I'm normally having dinner.

5 That's the hotel .... we stayed on our honeymoon.

6 This is the book .... I bought for Sue's birthday.

2 **Read the extract from a travel magazine about a Spanish festival called *La Tomatina*. Complete the gaps with *who, which, that, where, when* or *whose*.**

La Tomatina

Many of us have heard of La Tomatina, *the tomato-throwing festival* **(1)** .... *is held in Spain each summer – but what really goes on there? Reporter Sue King tells us more …*

La Tomatina is a celebration **(2)** .... people take part in the world's largest tomato fight. It takes place on the last Wednesday of August, **(3)** .... it starts with the *palo jamón*. The aim of this fun activity is to climb to the top of a pole **(4)** .... is covered in slippery grease. The leg of ham on top is the prize for the person **(5)** .... can reach it without sliding back down the pole or falling off. When someone finally grabs the ham, the tomato fight begins. Trucks full of tomatoes enter the town square, **(6)** .... they are then thrown at the crowd. These tomatoes come from an area of Spain called Extremadura, **(7)** .... they are grown specifically for the festival. The estimated number of tomatoes used in the fight is around 150,000. After exactly one hour, **(8)** .... shots are fired from water cannons, the fight ends. The square **(9)** .... the fight has taken place is then washed down and the participants, **(10)** .... bodies and faces are now covered in tomato paste, are also provided with water to clean themselves up. See you there next year?!

Speaking

Discussion ▶ CB page 105

1 **Read the exam questions and match two of them with the candidates' answers, A and B, below.**

1 Fewer people are reading books these days. Why do you think this is?

2 How important do you think it is to read stories to a young child? Why?

3 When a film has been made from a book, do you think it's better to see the film or read the book first? Why?

4 Many people read eBooks these days. Do you think this is a good development? Why/Why not?

A

Anna: OK, let me think. You know, I'm not really sure. Sometimes, **(1)** .... me, it's better to read the book first. That's **(2)** .... I get my own pictures in my head about the characters. What **(3)** .... you, Ben?

Ben: Yes, I like to read the book. The **(4)** .... is that a book is not only about what happens, the story or plot – it's the way it's written, how the writer makes us imagine the pictures. A film is different.

Anna: I agree. **(5)** .... why I don't understand people who say 'It wasn't as good as the book'. I'm not sure we should compare them because they're different.

Ben: For **(6)** ...., the Harry Potter books and films. Children read and loved the books but they got pleasure from the films for different reasons.

Anna: You know, in my **(7)** ...., that's a special example. **(8)** .... you think that the books and films sort of led into each other?

Ben: That's a good point.

B

Eva: Wow! I feel very **(1)** .... about this. I think it's very important for parents to read to their children. It helps their imaginations to grow. When I was young, my mum read to me every night and I looked forward to it a lot. **(2)** .... do you feel about it, Jack?

Jack: I couldn't agree more. It also helps the relationship between parent and child. I **(3)** .... that because sometimes it's the only time in the day that they have the chance to have time together. But you're right. Reading **(4)** .... this helps children in so many ways. **(5)** .... example, my dad used to read me adventure stories and I loved them so much I couldn't wait to learn to read myself.

Eva: And you haven't stopped since! He's always got his head in a book!

2 ▶ 19 **Complete the discussions with the words in the box. Then listen and check.**

| A | about | because | Don't | for | instance |
| | opinion | reason | That's | | |

| B | For | How | like | say | strongly |

3 **Underline phrases in the dialogues in Activity 1 that are used to**

1 ask for opinions.

2 give opinions.

3 give reasons and examples.

Listening

Multiple choice ▶ CB page 106

1 ▶ 20 **Listen to people talking in eight situations. For questions 1–8, choose the best answer, A, B or C.**

1 You hear a man and a woman talking about a play. Why does the man apologise?

   A he missed the show completely

   B he forgot it started yesterday

   C he hasn't bought a ticket yet

2 You hear two friends talking about an art exhibition. Where was the exhibition?

   A in a hotel   **B** in a gallery   **C** in a road

3 You hear some travel information on the radio. What does the presenter warn people about?

   A There are delays to flights from Bournemouth.

   B There is a lot of traffic going to a car festival.

   C Drivers won't be able to use one of the roads.

4 You hear a man and a woman talking about a meal they had together. Why did the man have a bad stomach?

   A he ate too much

   B he's allergic to one type of fish

   C the fish wasn't fresh

5 You hear a man leave a voicemail message. Why is he leaving the message?

   A to make a suggestion

   B to make a request

   C to make an arrangement

6 You hear a man and a woman talking about a sculpture exhibition. How does the woman feel?

   A she regrets not going to the exhibition

   B she admires the town the exhibition was in

   C she dislikes long journeys outside London

7 You overhear two people talking about recommending an English book. What type of book is the man going to recommend?

   A a children's book

   B a book for English learners

   C a detective novel

8 You hear a man talking on a radio show about buying books online. What problem did he have with online buying?

   A he was overcharged

   B he was sent the wrong book

   C a book arrived in bad condition

Vocabulary

arts and culture ▶ CB page 107

1 **Read the clues to complete the crossword puzzle and find the word for 13 down.**

1 the lines of a play

2 a large group of people playing instruments

3 a long story

4 a practice for a play or concert

5 a part of a book

6 a person who plays music

7 a person in a book, film or play

8 a person who paints pictures

9 a person who directs a group of people playing instruments

10 when actors, singers or musicians compete to get a part in a show

11 the story of a book or film

12 actors need to learn these for a play or film

13 ....

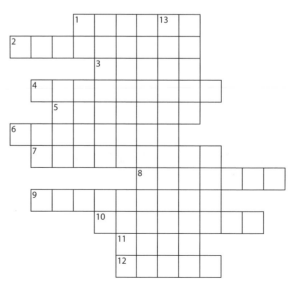

2 Complete the sentences with words from Activity 1.

1 I've lost my .... for the new play we're doing in drama club. Can I borrow yours?

2 The .... of the film is very complicated and I got confused towards the end.

3 Our school .... is going to play in a concert on TV next month.

4 I read the first three .... of the book but then I got bored and didn't finish it.

5 The main .... in *Romeo and Juliet* are from two families.

6 Ruth Rendell writes excellent detective ....

7 Janet is a very talented .... She plays the violin beautifully.

8 We've had five .... for the play but I still don't know all my ....

Grammar

articles ▶ CB page 108

1 Complete the sentences with *a*, *an*, *the* or – (no article).

1 Tina's going to live in .... Monte Carlo for a year – she's really looking forward to it.

2 I saw .... brilliant film last night!

3 Sue had .... headache yesterday so she didn't go to Mick's party. .... party was great fun, so it's a pity she missed it.

4 Hotpot is a dish from North West England made from .... potatoes and lamb.

5 I'm not usually into football but .... match I saw last night was really exciting.

6 Dan's going to .... North Pole next summer – how exciting is that?!

7 That's .... best play I've ever seen.

8 The town's annual music festival will be held in .... Brown Street this year.

9 This is .... third time Stacy's been to Scotland. She's from .... USA and she loves it here.

10 Jim's .... instructor at a golf course.

2 Complete the text about British food with *a*, *an*, *the* or – (no article).

BRITISH FOOD

Blo

I'm English, and I get a bit frustrated with the ideas people from other countries have about British food. Lots of visitors to **(1)** .... England end up going to fast food restaurants or eat in cheap places where **(2)** .... food isn't particularly good and then complain about it. I admit that in the past our meals weren't very exciting – lots of meat and potatoes, or greasy fish and chips. But these days we eat cuisine from all over **(3)** .... world. I bet you didn't know that **(4)** .... most popular dish in Britain is actually **(5)** .... dish called Tikka Masala from **(6)** .... India! It contains lots of tasty ingredients like **(7)** .... cream and spices and chicken. Italian food is popular too – you don't have to go far to find **(8)** .... excellent restaurant serving up everything from **(9)** .... pasta to seafood. But there *are* one or two traditional English meals that even people who aren't British love. How can you beat **(10)** .... big plateful of bacon, eggs, sausages and tomatoes for breakfast, or some delicious roast beef for lunch?

Use of English

Multiple-choice cloze ▶ CB page 109

1 Choose the correct alternative to complete the sentences.

1 I *made/did* so many mistakes in my German homework that my teacher said I had to *do/make* it again.

2 Jed's *done/made* a lot of money by working really hard. He's really *making/doing* his best in his job.

3 I *did/made* Ahmed a favour by *doing/making* his project for him but we got into trouble at school.

4 Steve hates Peter because he's always *making/doing* trouble. I told him to *do/make* an excuse and walk away whenever he tries to talk to him.

5 You've got to *do/make* the most of whatever situation you find yourself in. There's no point just *doing/making* a wish and hoping it will all go away.

6 The people outside were *doing/making* so much noise that I couldn't *make/do* the test properly.

2 Read the article again. For questions 1–8, decide which answer (A, B, C or D), best fits each gap. There is an example at the beginning (0).

Breaking a leg is good luck!

Well, that's what they say in the theatre, at **(0)** _least_ . Actors often wish each other good luck by saying 'Break a leg' before they go on stage and **(1)** .... on opening nights. They believe that it's _bad_ luck to say 'Good luck' but no one really knows why!

Another theatrical superstition (a belief that a certain action will **(2)** .... in something bad happening) is that actors should not

(3) .... 'the Scottish play' – Shakespeare's _Macbeth_. Actors are **(4)** .... something unpleasant will occur if they say the name of the play in the theatre. There are several possible **(5)** .... for this superstition. One is that there are a lot of sword **(6)** .... in the play – and the more they are practised, the more **(7)** .... it is there will be an injury. Another **(8)** .... is that the actor who was going to play Macbeth in the first ever performance died shortly before it began.

0	**A** least	**B** last	**C** once	**D** most
1	**A** really	**B** definitely	**C** absolutely	**D** especially
2	**A** start	**B** produce	**C** result	**D** take place
3	**A** mention	**B** observe	**C** notice	**D** tell
4	**A** believed	**B** influenced	**C** convinced	**D** proved
5	**A** causes	**B** explanations	**C** accounts	**D** reports
6	**A** plays	**B** arguments	**C** struggles	**D** fights
7	**A** likely	**B** possibly	**C** suitably	**D** clearly
8	**A** instruction	**B** approach	**C** advice	**D** suggestion

Writing

Article ▶ CB page 110

1 Read the exam task and the two candidates' answers. Both are grammatically correct but one is a better answer than the other. Which one? Think about these things.

length   opening sentence   range of vocabulary
structure   title

You have seen the following announcement in an international magazine.

We are going to publish a series of articles about great writers or artists from around the world. Who is your favourite writer, painter, musician, etc.? Send us your article and we'll include the best ones in the series.

Write your **article**.

A

An easy choice!

I know I should choose an artist from my own country – and we've got plenty to choose from! But I'm going to be different and go for a writer from another country, who I think was the best writer in the world! My choice is William Shakespeare.

As we all know, Shakespeare was English and he wrote a lot of plays and poems in the sixteenth century. We don't know a lot about his life but his work is read, performed and studied all over the world. Everyone has heard of Shakespeare, haven't they?

There are several reasons that I have chosen Shakespeare. Firstly, although he wrote a long time ago, his plays are still relevant now. We can still learn from them about human nature. Secondly, he gave the English language an enormous amount of new words and phrases that are still used today.

I find it amazing that people in India, Iraq and New Zealand all love and perform Shakespeare. He seems to speak to all people from all backgrounds, and that is why he is my favourite writer.

B

William Shakespeare

I have chosen William Shakespeare as my favourite writer. He is not from my country but from another. I think he was the best writer in the world.

Shakespeare was from England. People all over the world know his plays and poems. However, we do not have a lot of information about his own life.

Shakespeare's plays are important for people today. They are about human nature and everyone can learn something from them. He invented a lot of new words which have become part of the English language.

He is my favourite writer because lots of people from different countries like his work. He is really international.

2 Write your own answer to the task in Activity 1.

Style and design

11

Listening

Multiple matching ▶ CB page 112

1 ▶ **21** **Listen to five people talking about moving to a new home. Which speakers live in a house and which in a flat?**

2 ▶ **21** **Listen again. For questions 1–5, decide from the list (A–H) what each speaker dislikes about his/her new home. There are three extra letters you do not need to use.**

A the way the building is heated
B space to store things
C the floor covering
D the small garden
E the modern gadgets
F the view
G the countryside surroundings
H the lack of privacy

Speaker 1 ☐
Speaker 2 ☐
Speaker 3 ☐
Speaker 4 ☐
Speaker 5 ☐

Vocabulary

fashion and design ▶ CB page 113

1 **Choose one word in each group that does NOT fit.**

1	baggy	fitted	leather	short-sleeved	tight
2	cotton	fur	plain	silk	velvet
3	checked	flowery	loose	spotted	striped

2 **Choose the correct alternative to complete the sentences.**

1 People in cold countries often wear *cotton/fur* clothes to keep them warm.
2 This shirt is too *tight/loose*, I can hardly breathe!
3 You'll need a *silk/leather* jacket if you go on Jim's motorbike.
4 I used to wear red and white *plain/striped* pyjamas when I was a child.
5 I don't like the *material/shape* of this dress – it's too thin.
6 In the hot weather you'll need to have some *fitted/short-sleeved* T-shirts.

adjective order

3 **Put the adjectives in brackets in the correct order to complete the sentences.**

1 The bride wore a _____, _____, _____ (white, silk, long) wedding dress.

2 My mum hated my new _____, _____, _____ (leather, tight, black) trousers.

3 We used to have some horrible _____, _____, _____ (velvet, purple, floor-length) curtains in our old house.

4 In the school play I had to wear a _____, _____, _____ (cotton, checked, short-sleeved) cowboy shirt.

5 My favourite item of clothing at the moment is my _____, _____, _____ (leather, fitted, red) jacket.

6 My dad gave me a _____, _____, _____ (silk, plain, blue) tie to wear at the meeting.

4 **Complete the sentences with the words in the box.**

| classic | conscious | designer | fake |
| fashionable | genuine | | |

1 My aunt likes to be _____ and spends a lot of money on clothes.

2 It that a _____ leather bag? It must have cost a lot.

3 For kids today the name is more important than the look and they spend a lot of money on _____ clothes.

4 My dad isn't very fashion _____ and he still wears clothes he bought when he was a teenager!

5 They're not made of real fur, don't worry. They're _____ .

6 The design of that suit is a real _____ and will never go out of fashion.

Grammar
modals of possibility and certainty
▶ CB page 114

1 **Match sentences 1–8 with guesses A–H.**

1 Steffi has written a book about fashion.

2 Whenever I wear this top, I get a nasty rash.

3 Is Henry always so rude to people he doesn't know?

4 I didn't get onto the fashion course I wanted.

5 I've been calling the museum all day but nobody ever answers.

6 I can't find my ticket to the fashion show anywhere.

7 Gemma's been filming a make-up commercial since 6.30 this morning.

8 Look at the price of these boots – £500!

A You might have left it in the kitchen. I think I saw it there earlier.

B Well, they might be closed for the day. Have you checked the opening times?

C Poor you! You must be so disappointed.

D She must be exhausted.

E She must know a lot about the subject.

F That can't be right – they must have made a mistake!

G Mm, you must be allergic to the material.

H Not usually, you must have seen him on a bad day.

2 **Complete the email with _must_, _can't_ or _might_ and the correct form of the verbs in brackets.**

Hi, Jim

How are you? I've been really busy. My college organised a fashion show last week to raise money for charity. It was great fun. It **(1)** _____ (_take_) ages for the fashion students to make all the clothes. And the music department **(2)** _____ (_work_) really hard to create the music they put together for it. They asked me to be one of their models, which was great fun. They **(3)** _____ (_be_) bothered about what people looked like because I'm nothing like a model! But it was cool to be asked, and everyone who joined in did really well, so the organisers **(4)** _____ (_feel_) really proud.

The only disadvantage was that I wore my favourite shoes but I don't know where they are now. I **(5)** _____ (_leave_) them in the changing rooms at college, or maybe at a friend's house – I stayed there afterwards. The college **(6)** _____ (_expect_) so many people to turn up on the night because there weren't enough chairs in the hall and loads of people had to stand at the back to watch. They sold everything, though and raised a few hundred pounds – well, it **(7)** _____ (_be_) a thousand, I'm not sure. Anyway, they **(8)** _____ (_make_) so much money at a college event before!

I've attached a picture of me so you can see how funny I looked.

Write back and tell me all your news!

Mark

Use of English
Word formation ▶ CB page 115

1 Change the words in the box into nouns or adjectives by adding a suffix. You may need to make some spelling changes before adding the endings.

able	account	appear	assist	attract	bake
celebrate	dark	dirt	educate	fit	flexible
hunger	offend	please	sleep		

1 -ance   ....
2 -ion   ....
3 -y   ....
4 -ive   ....
5 -ness   ....
6 -ity   ....
7 -ant   ....
8 -(r)y   ....

2 Read the text below. Use the word given in capitals at the end of the line to form a word that fits in the gap in the same line. There is an example at the beginning (0).

My (bad) experience of a TV talent show

Last year I was a **(0)** _participant_ in a TV talent show called *You Got It!* I was excited about **(1)** .... the competition and turned up for the auditions at a local theatre. **(2)** ...., the judges loved what I did – I'm an acrobat – and they invited me back for the next round. But as I left the stage, I was **(3)** .... surrounded by the contestants who hadn't got through. I couldn't believe how **(4)** .... they were! I got nasty comments from them and they made **(5)** .... that I was no good. It wasn't very nice but I didn't want it to put me off. **(6)** ...., I passed the next audition too and went on to show the public my act live on TV. My **(7)** .... was going well until I slipped on stage and hurt my ankle and that was the end of it. It was such a **(8)** .... but I'm going to try again next year.

PARTICIPATE

ENTER
FORTUNE

SUDDEN

PLEASE

SUGGEST

LUCK

PERFORM

DISAPPOINT

Reading
Gapped text ▶ CB pages 116–117

1 Read the article quickly. How do you think the writer feels about the new store?

2 Read the article again. Six sentences have been removed. Choose from sentences A–G the one which best fits each gap. There is one extra sentence which you do not need to use.

A Even more temptation awaits as you finish paying.

B There is ample and easy parking for the drivers and a crèche for young babies while you wander round the store.

C Many young families today furnish their new homes completely from IKEA and are proud of the stylish tables, beds and sofas that furnish their rooms.

D Putting the furniture together can sometimes be annoying and take a lot of time.

E No one could imagine the success that this company would have.

F One of these is its commitment to helping the environment.

G Nearly all its stores have an identical layout.

3 Match the underlined words in the article with definitions 1–8.

1 a quick way to get somewhere   ....
2 first   ....
3 wonderful   ....
4 annoyed   ....
5 replaces itself naturally   ....
6 traffic jams   ....
7 items that are not necessary but decorative or useful   ....
8 fight   ....

A long-awaited arrival!

Karen Brindly writes about a famous newcomer to her area.

An important event took place in my local town recently, which has excited many local people and <u>irritated</u> others! It was first promised four or five years ago and since then people have been waiting for its arrival, uncertain whether it would have a positive or negative effect on the community. Was this a <u>stunning</u> piece of public art? Or perhaps a new rail link or extension to the airport? No. It was the opening of that very famous store with the widely recognised blue and yellow flag – a branch of the super chain store, IKEA.

IKEA, for those who may still be unaware of its global significance, is a Swedish furniture company that has more than 300 stores in 38 different countries. Started by Ingvar Kamprad in 1943, it is now the biggest furniture retailer in the world and few families in Europe and America are untouched by its business. **(1)** .... Even the art on their walls and china cups in the kitchen may have been bought there.

So, what are the reasons behind IKEAS's success? Undoubtedly, one is the fact that most of the furniture items that IKEA sells are in flat packs, ready for people to build themselves. **(2)** .... However, the idea of selling furniture this way was to reduce the energy costs of transport. Flat packs take up much less space than big tables and bookcases and it's better for the environment too.

In addition to this, IKEA try to make the shopping experience as enjoyable and stress free as possible for all involved. **(3)** .... And when you've finished shopping (in my case, absolutely exhausted), having spent much more than you <u>originally</u> intended, you can eat delicious Swedish meatballs and chips in the cafeteria!

Another reason for the store's success is its very clever in-store design. **(4)** .... You start on the top floor and follow a one way system that takes you past a range of furniture and <u>accessories</u> for every type of room. So, if you're looking for a new bed, you have to go past the kitchens, dining rooms and living rooms first! If you know what you're looking for, this can be extremely annoying! It's also confusing if, like me, you try to find a <u>short cut</u> to where you're going and end up lost, passing the same sofas and chairs again and again! Those meatballs in the cafeteria are definitely well-earned.

Having relaxed in the cafeteria, you are now ready to move downstairs. First, you pass through the area where you pick up your flat packs. If you manage to survive the crowds of people struggling to push trolleys filled with awkward packs of furniture, you reach the queues for the checkouts. There you start to worry that maybe, just maybe, you might have overspent. **(5)** .... Beyond the checkouts is a small food shop where you can buy even more meatballs (to eat at home) and other Swedish delicacies.

IKEA has a lot of good points. **(6)** .... In spite of being the world's third largest consumer of wood, its plan is to run the business using <u>renewable</u> energy as far as possible. It intends to build wind farms in Sweden and use solar panels in all its stores. It also contributes greatly to the economy of any town or city where it has a store. So, will it be a welcome addition to our local community? We shall just have to <u>battle</u> through the traffic <u>congestion</u> outside the store and see for ourselves.

Grammar

so, such, very; too, enough ▶ CB page 118

1 **Choose the correct alternative to complete the sentences.**

1 Wow! That was amazing! I've never seen *such/so* a good exhibition.

2 We're having our house designed by an award-winning architect – it's *so/such* expensive, we'll be paying for it 'til we retire!

3 There was a huge storm last night and all the lights went out at home. It was *so/such* dark we had to light candles.

4 I've broken your favourite mug. I'm *so/such* sorry! I'll buy you a new one.

5 I saw *such/so* an interesting programme on TV last night.

6 Denzel's been offered a place at university – he's done *such/so* well in his exams!

7 There was *so/such* excitement in the crowd outside the hotel – you just knew that someone really famous was about to turn up.

8 I'd love to study art and design at college, but it's just *so/such* hard to make a living when you graduate.

2 **Complete the customer feedback forms about a design exhibition. Use *very*, *too* or *enough*.**

1 The furniture designs were .... futuristic. I wouldn't mind having a piece in my home.

2 There weren't .... toilets in the venue – maybe you should choose another place next time!

3 I usually like looking at photos but there were .... many in this exhibition and you had to walk through them all to get to the next room.

4 My kids were .... pleased with the toy section – I'm bringing them again next time!

5 Great office furniture – I'd order some but it's .... expensive.

6 I didn't really enjoy this event – it was .... boring compared with last year's exhibition!

7 The place was certainly big .... to hold an exhibition like this, but it was cold and not very inviting.

8 We had to stand up to eat our lunch – there weren't .... places to sit in the café. Great show, though.

Speaking

question tags; personal information ▶ CB page 119

1 **Complete the questions with the correct tags.**

1 It's a gorgeous day today, ...?

2 We don't have to give in our homework until Friday, ...?

3 You really like designer clothes, ...?

4 This colour doesn't suit me, ...?

5 The film hasn't started yet, ...?

6 They won't build a new factory here, ...?

7 Jack is coming over later, ...?

8 You'll help me with this homework, ...?

2 ▶ 22 **Read the dialogues and choose the correct alternative to complete the questions. Listen and check.**

1 **A:** How do you like to spend your *free time/weekends*?
   B: I usually go out with friends or read a book. I enjoy reading. Sometimes at the weekends, I work out at the gym.

2 **A:** Would you say that you are a *punctual/trendy* person?
   B: I think so. I like to buy the latest designer clothes. When I've got enough money! And I keep up-to-date by reading magazines.

3 **A:** How important is your *mobile phone/laptop*?
   B: Oh – very. I couldn't live without it! I call or text my friends all the time and I keep all my mates' addresses and numbers on it too.

4 **A:** What was the *best/last* film you went to see?
   B: I haven't seen anything for a while. But I think it was something with Will Smith in. It had really good special effects but I can't remember the name.

3 **Read this extract from a speaking test and find and correct the grammatical mistakes. There are two mistakes in each of the candidate's answers.**

Examiner:	Where are you from, Anna?
Anna:	I'm from the Poland. I live in the Warsaw. It is an important city in my country.
Examiner:	And you, Katya?
Katya:	I am coming from Russia. My town is very big. I live in big house with my family.
Examiner:	What do you like about living in Warsaw, Anna?

Anna: I am like the people in my town. They are very friendly. The cold and snow aren't good, though! It is always freezing in winter. We must to wear fur coats and thick boots.

Examiner: And what about you, Katya?

Katya: My town is very pretty. Outside my town there are many trees and nice lakes. There are a lot of things for doing in the evening, too. Cafés, restaurants, walkings in the parks. I like my town very much.

Writing

Review ▶ CB page 120

1 Read the exam task and the candidate's answer and answer these questions.

1 What is the exhibition of?

2 Where is it?

3 What does it show?

4 Why was it interesting for the writer?

> You recently saw this notice on an international website.
>
> > If you have recently been to an interesting fashion or design exhibition, we would like to hear from you. Write a review of the exhibition, send it to us and we'll post it on our site.
>
> Write your review in **120–180** words.

2 Complete the review with the words in the box.

advice   display   favourites   how   However
particularly   reason   thoroughly

3 Read the review again and decide which instruction 1–6 the writer has NOT followed.

1 Write about a recent exhibition you have seen.

2 Divide your review into clear paragraphs.

3 Say what it was and why you went.

4 Explain what you can see at the exhibition.

5 Give your personal reaction.

6 Include a recommendation.

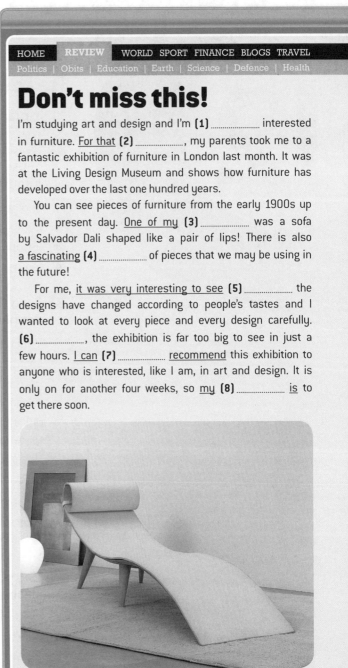

HOME **REVIEW** WORLD SPORT FINANCE BLOGS TRAVEL
Politics | Obits | Education | Earth | Science | Defence | Health

Don't miss this!

I'm studying art and design and I'm **(1)** .... interested in furniture. For that **(2)** ...., my parents took me to a fantastic exhibition of furniture in London last month. It was at the Living Design Museum and shows how furniture has developed over the last one hundred years.

You can see pieces of furniture from the early 1900s up to the present day. One of my **(3)** .... was a sofa by Salvador Dali shaped like a pair of lips! There is also a fascinating **(4)** .... of pieces that we may be using in the future!

For me, it was very interesting to see **(5)** .... the designs have changed according to people's tastes and I wanted to look at every piece and every design carefully. **(6)** ...., the exhibition is far too big to see in just a few hours. I can **(7)** .... recommend this exhibition to anyone who is interested, like I am, in art and design. It is only on for another four weeks, so my **(8)** .... is to get there soon.

4 Write your own review, using as many of the underlined phrases as you can.

Science and discovery

Reading

Multiple matching ▶ CB pages 122–123

1 Read the article about young female scientists and how they chose their careers. Match the women A–D with their jobs or intended jobs 1–4.

1 engineer ....
2 botanist ....
3 astrophysicist ....
4 forensic scientist ....

2 Read the article again. For questions 1–10, choose from people A–D. The people may be chosen more than once.

Which scientist

changed her attitude towards science at school?	**1**
once experimented on something that wasn't hers?	**2**
has a job in the media?	**3**
didn't get a lot of encouragement at school?	**4**
became interested in a fictional TV story?	**5**
considered several different careers?	**6**
followed a family trend?	**7**
was influenced by an expert on television?	**8**
chose to study something related to her free time interest?	**9**
didn't do what her parents expected her to do?	**10**

3 Match the words and phrases from the article 1–6 with meanings A –F.

1 convinced   A keen and enthusiastic
2 knowledgeable   B very sure
3 see much point in   C win
4 dedicated   D leave university early
5 pick up   E know a lot of facts
6 drop out   F understand the value of

Scientists today

Four of our best young female scientists talk about why they decided to follow a scientific path.

A Ruth

Today, I absolutely love science and I cannot imagine doing a job that wasn't related to it. However, that hasn't always been the case. When I was younger, I used to hate science lessons. Our science teacher was very clever and knowledgeable but he wasn't much good with children and he wasn't a good motivator. For me, science was hard and I couldn't really see much point in studying it. Then I started watching an American TV drama series about forensics, where the scientists are like detectives and work out how a person died. I found that really interesting and started to see my science lessons in a different way. Now I'm studying forensic science at university and loving every minute of it!

B Gabriella

Both my parents are scientists and they work in research, developing new medicines and vaccines. They're completely dedicated to their work and this has obviously had an effect on their children. My elder brother won a science scholarship to go to a top university to study physics and since then he's picked up several prizes for things he has invented. I went in a different direction and found that I loved botany. I used to spend hours in our garden planting and growing strange flowers and trees! Now I give advice to gardeners and you can see me in my own TV show on Saturdays!

C Gemma

I liked a lot of different subjects at school and I was quite good at a wide range of things. So, it was hard to decide what I wanted to do as a career. First, I wanted to teach

geography, then I decided I didn't have enough patience to be a teacher. After that, I decided to do a sports degree because I loved swimming. I didn't enjoy the course, so I dropped out and became a personal trainer. Then, much to everyone's amazement, I applied to university to study an engineering degree in motor sports! I'd had a love of fast cars since I passed my driving test and driving cars was my big hobby in my late teens. It was a brilliant course. Now I work for one of the famous Formula 1 racing teams. It's a great life! A bit different to teaching geography!

D Diana

When I was young, my mum and dad were convinced that I was going to be an engineer. Unlike other children, I wasn't interested in books and stories or even playing with toys. What I was interested in was pulling everything apart to see how it worked. The problem was that I never put them back together again and I think that through the years I broke nearly everything I owned – and that other people owned too! I remember making my best friend cry because I took apart the new toy steam train that he'd just got for his birthday! So, it came as a surprise when I decided not to study engineering at university but to go for astrophysics instead! It's quite a long way from studying how things work to watching the stars and planets and learning all about what they're made of. But it all started when I saw the incredible scientist, Brian Cox, present a series of TV documentaries about the planets. He switched me on to the solar system and since then my head has literally been 'in the stars'!

Grammar

third conditional and *wish* ▶ CB page 124

1 **There is one word missing in each sentence. Find the missing word and add it to each sentence.**

1 If no one invented the mobile phone, we wouldn't have been able to send text messages.

2 I have gone to the science museum with you if I had known you were going.

3 I wish I come up with an invention that had changed the world – I'd be famous now!

4 If my parents hadn't bought me a telescope, I wouldn't become so interested in the stars.

5 If my friend Gary hadn't explained that experiment to me, I not have got a good mark in my physics homework.

6 I bet Toni wishes she gone to the talk – Professor Brian Cox was there!

7 If they hadn't invented the wheel, we not have developed motor vehicles.

8 I wish I not dropped out of university – I would have a degree by now.

2 **Complete the text using the correct form of the verbs in brackets.**

Use of English

Key word transformations ▶ CB page 125

1 **Choose the correct alternative to complete the sentences.**

1 An interesting topic *came up/came across* in our biology class today – we talked about new species of animals that scientists have discovered.

2 I'm finding it quite difficult to *look into/keep up with* geography at school. I don't understand the teacher very well.

3 The teacher *gave away/ran out of* the answers to the chemistry quiz by forgetting to cover them up, so we got them all right!

4 I wish Tamsin wouldn't keep *going on about/coming up with* getting a B in science – it's better than anyone else in the class got!

5 The plans for a new sports centre *gave away/fell through* because they didn't get permission to build on the land.

6 I *came across/kept up with* my old school reports yesterday – I'd forgotten I still had them!

Thank goodness they invented it!

In a recent survey we asked people which inventions they were most grateful for. Here's what some of them said.

Jenny, 35

I don't know what I **(1)** .... (*do*) if they **(2)** .... (*not invent*) satellite navigation for cars! I was never very good at using maps to find my way – my husband used to make fun of me when I rang him up because I'd got lost in the middle of nowhere – AGAIN! So, I decided to get a sat nav for my car, so I wouldn't have to ring him anymore. I

wish I **(3)** .... (*get*) one sooner because now I don't need to ask for directions. I've never told my husband I've got it – I just pretend I've become an expert map-reader!

Steve, 14

Computer games! I don't play them myself but my friends spend a lot of time at their computers while I'm out playing cricket. I've just been accepted into a sports academy where I'm going to improve my skills. If no one **(4)** .... (*come up with*) with computer games, perhaps I **(5)** .... (*have*) more competition from my mates on the sports field!

Tiffany, 21

Thank goodness they invented contact lenses. I've never minded wearing glasses – in fact, I've got some really trendy ones, but it can be hard work when it's raining – you can't see very well and they get all steamed up. If I **(6)** .... (*buy*) contacts sooner, I would have avoided some embarrassing situations. One day I walked up to a man who I thought was my boyfriend and gave him a hug! Fortunately, he thought it was quite funny so it was OK! In fact, he became a good friend. So if I **(7)** .... (*choose*) to get contacts sooner, I **(8)** .... (*miss*) the chance of a good friendship!

What are *you* glad has been invented?

2 **For questions 1–6, complete the second sentence so that it has a similar meaning to the first sentence, using the word given. Do not change the word given. You must use between two and five words, including the word given.**

Example: *She managed to open the door.*
IN
She succeeded in opening the door.

1 Jean told everyone about my secret invention.
AWAY
Jean .... secret invention to everyone.

2 I didn't pass my science exam because I didn't work hard enough.
HARDER
If .... for my science exam, I would have passed.

3 Steph keeps complaining about our new history teacher but I think he's OK.
GOING
Steph .... our new history teacher but I think he's OK.

4 I try hard to stay at the same speed as everyone in the running team but I just can't.
KEEP
I try hard to .... everyone in the running team but I just can't.

5 Scientists will discover a cure for cancer before too long.
FOUND
Scientists .... a cure for cancer before too long.

6 'I'm not coming to the party with you because I'm too tired.'
REFUSED
Carla .... to the party because she was too tired.

Listening

Multiple choice ▶ CB page 126

1 ▶ 23 **Listen to part of a radio interview. Who is speaking and what is his job?**

2 ▶ 23 **Listen again. For questions 1–7, choose the best answer (A, B or C).**

1 Jamie became a science teacher because he
  A felt that science was based on magic.
  B particularly enjoyed the subject at school.
  C was inspired by his own science teacher.

2 What does Jamie enjoy most about teaching science?
  A using helpful materials with his class
  B the interest that students have in the subject
  C the chance to see students find things out

3 What does Jamie say about the science subject he likes teaching most?
  A It is difficult for many students to understand.
  B The experiments are exciting to carry out.
  C It focuses on things that students easily recognise.

4 What does Jamie find most difficult about teaching?
  A seeing students struggle to understand things
  B experiencing bad behaviour in class
  C not having access to the right equipment in class

5 How does Jamie feel about his school's entry for the science fair?
  A concerned for the students that it might not win
  B confident that it will receive one of the top prizes
  C worried that other schools will come up with better ideas

6 Jamie thinks that it is important to teach science because
  A it gives students skills for their working lives.
  B it provides ongoing opportunities for discovery.
  C it is different to other school subjects.

7 Why does Jamie wish he had discovered a new kind of medicine?
  A He would have enjoyed being recognised for his work.
  B He would have liked to make a difference to people's lives.
  C He would have been happy to pass the information on to students.

Vocabulary

research and discovery; science and scientists ▶ CB page 127

1 **Match words 1–8 with meanings A–H.**

1 records
2 vaccine
3 conclusion
4 experiment
5 process
6 laboratory
7 research
8 discovery

A   a place where students learn about science

B   a scientific test

C   a procedure or method

D   work to find out more about a topic

E   something which prevents some illnesses

F   we keep these to refer to later if necessary

G   something you (or others) didn't know before

H   something you deduce from certain facts

2   Choose the correct alternative to complete the collocations in sentences 1–8.

1   Scientists have recently *made/done* an important discovery about possible life in the solar system.

2   We need to *survey/analyse* these results to see if our ideas were correct or not.

3   Kathy *came/went* up with an excellent idea for our new science project.

4   In the exam, we have to *drive/conduct* an experiment in the laboratory.

5   Did the doctor *take/make* an X-ray of your leg after the accident?

6   I've *got/reached* the conclusion that I am not very good at science!

7   I don't think I've *made/done* enough research to write my assignment yet.

8   They're hoping to *carry/develop* a vaccine that will prevent everyone from getting colds.

Grammar

reporting verbs ▶ CB page 128

1   Report statements and questions 1–6 using the reporting verbs in the box.

apologised	asked	offered	refused
reminded	warned		

1   'Would you like to be a scientist when you leave school?' my granddad said.
   My granddad _____ .

2   'Can I help you carry those boxes?' she said.
   She _____ .

3   'I'm not going to the awards ceremony' the scientist said.
   The scientist _____ .

4   'Remember to wear your goggles,' our teacher said.
   Our teacher _____ .

5   'Be careful! Some of those chemicals are dangerous!' she said.
   She _____ .

6   'I'm so sorry I missed the concert,' Mum said.
   Mum _____ .

Speaking

Collaborative task ▶ CB page 129

1   ▶24   Read the exam task and the extracts from a candidate's discussion. Complete the phrases they use to agree or disagree with the words in the box. Then listen and check.

Here are some different inventions that have been very important for us. Talk to each other about how these inventions have changed people's lives. Then decide which invention you think has been the most important.

1 light bulb	2 telephone	3 car
4 computer	5 spectacles	6 TV

disagree	more	partly	point	right	wouldn't

Extract A

A: The light bulb was important because it meant that people could stay up later!

B: I couldn't agree **(1)** _____ . It also meant that there weren't so many fires from candles and lamps.

A: You're absolutely **(2)** _____ .

Extract B

A: I don't think that spectacles were particularly important, do you? It didn't change the way people lived.

B: I **(3)** _____ say that. It helped a lot of people continue their jobs and enjoy their lives better.

A: OK. I agree up to a **(4)** _____ . But I don't think that invention was as important as, say, the light bulb.

Extract C

A: For me, the most important invention was the telephone. It let people contact each other from long distances.

B: I completely **(5)** _____ with you! In my opinion, it was the computer. Look how it's changed everybody's lives today.

A: I **(6)** _____ agree with you – but you see, without the telephone I don't think we would have the computer, would we?

B: OK. I see what you mean!

Long turn ▶ CB page 129

2 ▶ 25 Read the exam task and look at the pictures below. Read candidate A and B's answers and choose the correct alternatives. Then listen and check.

> **Student A:** Your pictures show people doing different jobs connected with science. Compare the pictures and say what might be interesting about doing the different jobs.
>
> **Student B:** Which job would you prefer?

A: OK. **(1)** *Both/Two* pictures show people who have got scientific jobs but the sort of jobs are very different. In the picture **(2)** *at/on* the left, an astronaut is out in space. I **(3)** *imagine/wonder* he's doing a space walk. They sometimes do this to repair the space ship. He **(4)** *must/might* have a lot of knowledge about science but he's doing a practical job. The man on the right, **(5)** *however/although*, is in a classroom or lecture room and he's teaching some students about science. He's showing them an experiment or something **(6)** *as/like* that. I don't think his job is as exciting **(7)** *than/as* the astronaut's because he's always in a classroom, **(8)** *whereas/despite* the astronaut goes to fantastic places. He can see things that not many people have seen. It's dangerous **(9)** *although/because* a lot of things **(10)** *must/can* go wrong, but I think it's more interesting than being a teacher!

B: I'd **(11)** *rather/prefer* to work in a classroom because I'd be **(12)** *especially/really* scared to be up in space!

Writing

Essay ▶ CB page 130

1 Complete the sentences with the linking words in the box.

> although   As a result   Despite   However
> In addition to this   In spite

1 Many students today are still not very interested in science .... teaching methods have got much better.

2 .... of the bad weather, the scientists continued with the experiment.

3 Billy failed all his science exams last year. ...., this year he passed them all.

4 We'll be visiting the Science Museum. ...., we'll have a tour of the Botanical Gardens.

5 .... of advances in medical science, we shall soon have a vaccine against many cancers.

6 .... learning problems when he was a child, the boy eventually became a famous inventor.

2 Read the exam task and the candidate's answer. Choose the correct alternatives to complete the essay.

> You have recently had a discussion about science in schools. Now your teacher has asked you to write an essay.
>
> **Essay question:**
> *Schools should timetable more science lessons. Do you agree?*
>
> **Notes:**
> Things to write about:
> 1   interest
> 2   careers
> 3   your own idea
> Write your essay in **140–190** words.

In my **(1)** *opinion/thought*, this is a very **(2)** *challenging/controversial* topic for most school children. **(3)** *While/When* some students who enjoy and are good at science subjects would be **(4)** *in/on* favour of more science lessons, there are many more who do not think it is a good idea.

I **(5)** *hope/understand* that science is very important and that we need to have good, young scientists to help our lives become easier and also to help us protect the planet. Those students who show interest in science when they are young, definitely need to be encouraged.

(6) *However/Although*, I do not think the answer is to increase the number of science lessons for everyone. I **(7)** *experience/feel* very strongly that there are lots of things young people need to do. We need to learn about music, art and books. **(8)** *In/As* addition to this, we need to do sport and learn how to keep healthy.

(9) *For/In* conclusion, I must **(10)** *point/say* that it is not the number of science lessons that is important, but how they are taught. We need good science teachers who can motivate the students. Then we'll get good scientists.

3 Write your own answer to the exam task.

Useful language

Invitations and apologies

1 **Match invitations 1–4 with responses A–D.**

1 I'm having a birthday party on Saturday. Would you like to come?

2 I'm going shopping later. Do you fancy coming with me?

3 I'm writing to invite you and Tom to our wedding on 8th July. Brian and I do hope you'll be able to come.

4 Jan and I are going to the new restaurant in Bridge Street for a meal on Thursday. Would you like to join us?

A I'd love to. I need to get some new shoes. Where shall we meet?

B Thank you so much for inviting us. We would love to come but unfortunately we'll be in the USA working for the whole summer.

C Thanks for asking me but I'm afraid I have to work late on Thursday. Have a great time!

D That would be great. Is it at your house? What time do you want people to arrive?

2 **Underline phrases in Activity 1 used for**

A inviting   **B** accepting   **C** thanking   **D** apologising

3 **Which invitation in Activity 1 is the most formal?**

Opinions and agreement

1 **Match sentences 1–10 with situations A–F below. Some situations have more than one sentence.**

1 I feel very strongly that students shouldn't have to pay for public transport.

2 I like this book, don't you?

3 I see what you mean, but I'm not too sure I agree.

4 Yes, I'm with you – up to a point.

5 So, what do you think about the new reality show?

6 I completely agree. The film was so boring.

7 In my opinion, the test was really hard! What did you think?

8 You're right. I totally agree.

9 I don't think it was a good match. How did you feel about it?

10 No, I don't think so.

A asking for an opinion

B asking for agreement

C giving an opinion

D expressing agreement

E expressing partial agreement

F expressing disagreement

Suggestions, recommendations and advice

1 **Complete conversations 1–6 with the correct form of the verbs in brackets.**

1 **A:** I'm having real problems deciding what to study at university. What would you advise me .... (*do*)?

B: If I were you, I'd .... (*talk*) to the career's advisor at school. She's really good.

2 **A:** I've got some visitors from Norway over for the weekend. Where do you recommend .... (*go*) for a meal?

B: I can thoroughly .... (*recommend*) the New Park Hotel. They serve some lovely traditional English food.

3 **A:** OK. So, we're doing this project about fashion together. Where do you suggest we .... (*start*)?

B: Why don't we .... (*do*) some research online about fashion trends? Then we can .... (*download*) some useful information.

4 **A:** I've had a terrible headache all day. What should I .... (*do*) about it?

B: I think you should .... (*get*) some sleep. You look really tired.

5 **A:** I'm staying In London for a few days. Any ideas about places .... (*visit*)?

B: How about .... (*go*) to an art exhibition at the National Gallery? There's usually something good on there. Or you could always .... (*go*) to one of the musicals in the West End.

6 **A:** We could .... (*get*) a good DVD to watch this weekend. Any suggestions?

B: Yes. Let's .... (*get*) the latest Harry Potter. We haven't seen that yet.

Requests, offers and permission

1 **Match conversations 1–8 with speakers A–H.**

1 **A:** <u>Could you</u> get me some water, please?

B: <u>Certainly</u>. <u>I'll bring</u> some immediately.

2 **A:** <u>I wonder if you could</u> help me. I'm looking for Trent Road.

B: <u>Sure</u>. Turn left just after the church.

3 **A:** Could I have a quick word? <u>Would you mind</u> checking this student's essay for me?

B: <u>No problem</u>.

4 **A:** <u>I'll deal with</u> this next customer if you like.

B: I'm not too busy now, so <u>it's OK. Thanks anyway</u>.

5 **A:** Sue, <u>can I</u> use your mobile for a moment? I left mine in Dad's car.

B: <u>That's fine</u>. Here you are.

6 **A:** <u>Would you like me to</u> carry that shopping to the car for you?

B: <u>That's very kind of you</u>.

7 **A:** <u>Is it OK if I</u> borrow the car tonight to go to Mack's party?

B: <u>Sorry</u>, not tonight. I'll be using it myself.

8 **A:** <u>Could you please</u> let me know about the job as soon as possible?

B: <u>Of course</u>. We'll contact you next week.

A two sales assistants

B a customer and a waiter

C two strangers in the street

D two teachers

E a future employee and employer

F teenager and parent

G two school friends

H supermarket assistant and customer

2 **Put the underlined phrases in Activity 1 under the correct heading.**

Requesting	**Responding to requests**
Can you …	I'm afraid I can't …
....	....
....	....
....	....
....	

Offering

Shall I do …

....

....

....

Responding to offers

Thanks. That's brilliant.

....

....

Asking for permission

May I …

....

....

Giving/Refusing permission

Yes, of course you may/can.

....

....

Useful phrases for the Speaking Exam

1 **Match the headings in the box with the groups of phrases 1–8.**

adding   asking for clarification
bringing your partner in
giving yourself some time to think
interrupting   organising the discussion
reminding   speculating

1 ....
Could you repeat that, please?
What exactly do you mean?
Are you saying that …

2 ....
Don't forget we have to …
You must remember to …

3 ....
Could I just say here that …
Excuse me, but I think …
Sorry to interrupt, but I …

4 ....
As well as that, I think that …
I'd like to add that …

5 ....
Let me think.
I haven't thought about that before.
That's an interesting question.

6 ....
Let's start by thinking about …
Shall we start here … ?
Shall we move onto … ?
We haven't discussed …, have we?
It's time we made a decision.

7 ....
So, what do you think?
Do you agree?
What happens in your country?
Have you got any experience of … ?

8 ....
I imagine that …
It looks as though …
It might be quite difficult to …
It would probably be better to …

Useful phrases for the Writing Exam

1 **Choose the phrase (A, B or C) which is the most formal in situations 1–6.**

1 Addressing a person in a letter or email
   A Dear Katy   **B** Hi, Pam   **C** Dear Sir

2 Signing off a letter or email
   A Love, Pete   **B** Best wishes, Mary   **C** Yours, Saul

3 Starting a letter or email
   A Great to hear from you.
   B It was kind of you to contact me.
   C Thanks for your last letter/email.

4 Giving a reason for writing
   A I'm writing to apply for the job advertised in the newspaper.
   B I'm writing to let you know I'll be back in London next month.
   C I'm writing to says thanks for such a lovely birthday present.

5 Referring to previous contact
   A I'm so happy to hear your news.
   B With reference to your previous letter, I …
   C You sounded a bit low in your last letter.

6 Closing a letter or email
   A Please write soon.
   B I hope to hear from you soon.
   C I look forward to hearing from you.

2 **Choose the type of writing task where you are most likely to find phrases 1–10.**

1 On the other hand   (essay/story)
2 How would you feel if …?   (article/report)
3 We had only just set off when …   (review/story)
4 It is widely believed that …   (story/essay)
5 It is based on a true story.   (review/essay)
6 It's definitely worth reading.   (review/story)
7 I would recommend a short visit to …   (essay/report)
8 The purpose of this report is to …   (report/article)
9 The plot is extremely exciting.   (story/review)
10 On balance, I believe that more people spend … (essay/story)

Practice tests

Paper 1 Reading and Use of English

Part 1

For questions **1–8**, read the text below and decide which word (**A**, **B**, **C** or **D**) best fits each gap. There is an example at the beginning (**0**).

Example

0   **A** requirement   **B** necessity   **C** want   **D** desire

Mark your answers **on the separate answer sheet**.

How to invent things

Inventions are created through (**0**) _necessity_, and this is the best (**1**) _____ of creating something. The first step is identifying a need – either someone (**2**) _____ there is a lack of something useful, or they decide life would be easier if only there was a device that would do a task more quickly. This is when creative people get (**3**) _____ and make the gadget for themselves. Another way to invent something is by observing other people (**4**) _____ to do something and concluding that there must be another way to get the (**5**) _____ done. This can occur by (**6**) _____ – you see someone slip on the ice and invent a new kind of snowshoe – or it can be deliberate. Perhaps you want to start up a business but you don't know what kind of product to (**7**) _____ on. So, you look for ideas. You see someone battling with a (**8**) _____ and come up with a way to make it easier – and bingo! Your invention is born.

1	**A** power	**B** method	**C** habit	**D** force
2	**A** realises	**B** suggests	**C** tells	**D** values
3	**A** busy	**B** alive	**C** keen	**D** fast
4	**A** arguing	**B** struggling	**C** concentrating	**D** competing
5	**A** exercise	**B** subject	**C** task	**D** question
6	**A** incident	**B** accident	**C** example	**D** instance
7	**A** plan	**B** attempt	**C** direct	**D** focus
8	**A** problem	**B** matter	**C** trouble	**D** factor

Part 2

For questions **9–16**, read the text below and think of the word which best fits each gap. Use only **one** word in each gap. There is an example at the beginning (**0**).

Write your answers **IN CAPITAL LETTERS on the separate answer sheet**.

Example

0	B	E	E	N

Weather and mood

For decades, researchers have **(0)** _been_ trying to establish whether there is a relationship between weather and mood. **(9)** ...., despite the various studies that have been carried out, researchers can't agree. While some studies say that the weather has only a small effect on mood, others say weather conditions can affect us significantly – including humidity, temperature and sunshine. **(10)** .... to these studies, humid conditions make us feel sleepy and make **(11)** .... harder to concentrate, whereas higher temperatures lower feelings of anxiety. Unsurprisingly, the higher the number of sunshine hours we experience, the **(12)** .... optimistic we feel.

Psychologists, **(13)** .... course, believe it's up to us to create positive experiences **(14)** .... ourselves, whatever the weather. So, when the rain **(15)** .... falling we should listen to music, read a good book or do some exercise. If the sun is shining, we should get out there and take advantage of the lightness **(16)** .... increases our serotonin levels – a natural, feel-good chemical that makes us feel awake and happy.

The Red Bulletin magazine

Part 3

For questions **17–24**, read the text below. Use the word given in capitals at the end of some of the lines to form a word that fits in the gap in the same line. There is an example at the beginning (**0**).

Write your answers **IN CAPITAL LETTERS on the separate answer sheet**.

Example

0	S	T	R	E	S	S	F	U	L

Going on holiday: Why do we bother?

Going on holiday can be **(0)** _stressful_ and it starts before you even leave home.	**STRESS**
The list of things to do is **(17)** .... and it isn't too long before your	**END**
(18) .... starts to run out. Eventually, however, the bags are packed and you're off for some fun.	**PATIENT**
Or are you? You **(19)** .... arrive at your destination only to find the hotel's	**FINAL**
a building site, the air-conditioning is **(20)** .... and it's all very noisy. The hotel	**BREAK**
(21) .... is run by idiots and your kids come down with food poisoning. And then	**ENTERTAIN**
there's the journey home. The flight is **(22)** .... and your luggage gets lost.	**DELAY**
So, why do we do it? I often find myself **(23)** .... whether holidays are worth	**WONDER**
the effort. Yet I still find it **(24)** .... to look at the photos I've uploaded onto the	**EXCITE**
computer, and I can't help having a quick browse on the internet for ideas for next year's trip. It's all good fun really.	

Part 4

For questions **25–30**, complete the second sentence so that it has a similar meaning to the first sentence, using the word given. **Do not change the word given**. You must use between two and five words, including the word given.

Here is an example (**0**)

Example

0   'I'm really sorry that I broke your new phone,' Belle said.

APOLOGISED

Bella .... my new phone.

The gap can be filled by 'apologised for breaking', so you write:

0 | APOLOGISED FOR BREAKING

Write **IN CAPITAL LETTERS on the separate answer sheet**.

---

25   'I don't like this pizza,' said Vicky.
KEEN
Vicky said she .... the pizza.

26   Michael can't swim very well.
AT
Michael .... swimming.

27   Karl made me jump when he suddenly walked into the room.
TOOK
Karl .... when he suddenly walked into the room.

28   They're building a new sports centre in the town.
BUILT
A new sports centre .... in the town.

29   The entry ticket to the fair includes one free ride.
IS
One free ride .... the entry ticket to the fair.

30   'Remember to lock the door when you leave,' Mum told me.
REMINDED
Mum .... the door when I left.

Part 5

You are going to read a newspaper article about a festival called *Carnevale* which takes place each winter in Venice, Italy. For questions **1–6**, choose the answer (**A**, **B**, **C** or **D**) which you think fits best according to the text.

Mark your answers **on the separate answer sheet**.

Venetian Masquerade

Last month Liz Ford put on a mask and set off for Carnevale, *Venice's popular mid-winter festival.*

At carnival time in Italy's watery city, wearing a mask appears to be a compulsory part of the uniform. So, when I attended the carnival last month with my friend, Asha, we decided it was something that we too had to put on. We browsed the stalls lining the streets selling what has become the symbol of the carnival. But as there were literally hundreds to choose from, it didn't make for an easy decision and I wasn't satisfied until I had finally settled on one with a few decorative feathers and was ready to take part in the festivities.

The people of Venice have been celebrating *Carnevale* since the fifteenth century. In those days, parties were arranged where rich and poor alike hid their identity behind masks and danced the nights away to forget the difficulties of winter. The tradition gradually faded away until, in 1979, it was brought back to life, becoming one of the world's most popular festivals. Today, however, some of the city's residents complain that the carnival is nothing compared to its former self, and is purely geared towards bringing in money.

The festivities begin with *La Festa delle Marie*, a parade through the city and a taste of what is to come. Throughout the following days, guests attend fabulous masked balls, where they mingle with others, watch acrobats and artists and dine on delightful food and drink – the carnival is truly a feast for the senses. The highlight of the festival is without doubt the Grand Masked Ball, located in a beautiful palace and a chance to show off your knowledge of Venetian traditions, such as performing the steps of the ancient *quadrilles* dances. That won't be me, then!

My friend, Asha and I spent our days in Venice exploring the narrow waterways, hidden shops and cafés. The bustling crowds and party atmosphere were electrifying but without doubt the highlight of our trip was dressing for a special dinner on our final night. We put on our masks, hired dresses and no longer felt out of place with the other party-goers. We boarded the boat at St Mark's bay, lit by street lamps. As the gondola swept up canals past ancient buildings in the shadows of night, I noticed an air of mystery that hadn't been revealed during daylight. Somebody on board passed around sparklers and we waved the fiery sticks at onlookers as we passed under bridges. Putting on a mask makes you an instant hit at carnival time.

Leaving the boat in San Polo we headed for dinner. Walking into the candlelit restaurant was like stepping back in time. More than 50 people were already seated, every face hidden behind a mask, just as they would have been centuries ago. At first, I found it difficult talking to people I couldn't see properly, though I soon started enjoying myself. The entertainment, provided by modern dancers, wasn't quite of the era the feast was meant to represent. But the food was superb and the setting magnificent.

After our meal, Asha and I went out into the busy streets again and found our way to a jazz bar which, though it played more popular music than jazz, was the ideal place to finish off our stay in Venice. As dawn broke, the party carried on, but we sadly made our way towards the *vaporetto*, the Venetian waterbus which all too quickly carried us along the canals towards the airport for our morning flight back to London. We finally took off our masks – the party was over for me and Asha – but I hope we'll be back next year.

1   When talking about carnival masks, the writer says that

   A   she felt relieved when she had chosen one to wear.

   B   they are the reason why many people go to the celebration.

   C   it was strange to see such large numbers of people wearing them.

   D   she would have preferred not to have to wear one.

2   According to the writer, some people feel that today's *Carnevale*

   A   draws people's attention away from bad weather.

   B   doesn't deserve its international reputation.

   C   is simply a money-making scheme.

   D   is better than it used to be.

3   What does *a feast for the senses* mean in line 13?

   A   something that is delicious to eat

   B   something that is pleasing to experience

   C   something that is unexpected

   D   something that provides a chance to meet people

4   As the writer went out on the final evening of her stay, she

   A   was pleased to be wearing a suitable costume.

   B   was embarrassed by the attention she received from spectators.

   C   was impressed with the way the streets had been decorated.

   D   was surprised that the city looked so strange at night.

5   What comment does the writer make about the dinner she attended?

   A   The food was disappointing.

   B   The location was too dark.

   C   The customers were unfriendly.

   D   The entertainment was unusual.

6   In the final paragraph, the writer

   A   feels confident that she will be back in Venice in the near future.

   B   is unimpressed with the transport which she has to use.

   C   is disappointed with the way the last evening finishes.

   D   expresses regret at having to leave the party.

Part 6

You are going to read a magazine article about climbing Everest. Six sentences have been removed from the article. Choose from the sentences **A–G** the one which fits each gap (**7–12**). There is one extra sentence which you do not need to use.

Mark your answers **on the separate answer sheet**.

Climbing Everest

Mountaineer and author, Andy Cave, explains its beautiful, fatal attraction ...

It hurts. Anybody who climbs above 8,000m without oxygen and says it doesn't is a liar. I take six steps and then bend over my ice axe, resting my head in the snow. Babu Chiri Sherpa and my fellow-climber David are doing exactly the same. A few minutes later, we are standing on the very top of Shishapangma (8,013m), exhausted but very happy. The white mountains of the Himalaya run off to the curved horizon, dividing the green hills of Nepal and the endless desert of Tibet. You can see the giant, Everest, to the east.

Why does Everest continue to attract people? **7** Look at portraits of climbers returning from the summit of Everest; look at the triumph on their faces. Yes, they also look tired. The combination of sun, wind and cold has roughened their skin and they will be dehydrated. More than anyone, they understand the risks involved and they look relieved to be back on firm ground.

The truth is that the thought of standing on the highest point of the earth (8,840m) is a dream for many climbers. And not just a dream. **8** In the spring of 2009 alone, 338 people reached the summit, some of them with little mountaineering experience.

In recent years, for various reasons, the chances of climbing the peak successfully have improved considerably. There are several reasons for this. Firstly, above 8,000m on Everest, almost everyone breathes bottled oxygen and the bottles used now are much lighter than their predecessors. Secondly, the clothing available for today's mountaineers is made with sophisticated designs and hi-tech fabrics and the weight of equipment such as crampons and karabiners has been dramatically reduced.

To climb on Everest is to walk through history, myth and legend. The achievement of Hillary, Tenzing and team making the first ascent in 1953, is well-known to all of us, but the real romance and mystery is reserved for the story of George Mallory and Andrew Irvine in 1924. The two men were attempting Everest from Tibet via the North Col. **9**

Every climber has a view on the fate of Mallory and Irvine, on whether or not they reached the summit. In 1999, American alpinist Conrad Anker found Mallory's body on the north side of Everest, but without his camera. **10** His partner Irvine's body has never been recovered.

The normal route up Everest, via the South Col, is not a technically difficult climb by today's standards, but it still commands respect. In 1996, a single storm killed eight people and it made no difference whether they were inexperienced mountaineers or sherpas. In the spring of 2009, five people died on the mountain. Mountaineers have to accept the risks involved and put in place strategies to reduce these risks. **11**

For many, climbing Everest will be considered pointless, but its attraction will never die.

12 To climb any mountain is to take a risk. If human beings had always played safe, we'd all be sitting in caves, living like animals. Perhaps George Mallory understood the motivation of most climbers when he wrote, 'What we get from this adventure is sheer joy. And joy is, after all, the end of life. We do not live to eat and make money.'

A This is unfortunate as scientists believe that the film could have been developed, which might have solved the mystery.

B Perhaps the desire to climb so high is part of the human desire to explore and to push the boundaries.

C The last known sighting of them was on 8th June, through a gap in the clouds, just a few hundred metres from the summit.

D However, there is also a longing to enjoy the moment before returning to routine daily life.

E Good ones go bravely into the mountains, not blindly.

F Although the media seem obsessed with the risk and loss associated with mountain climbing, clearly this is not what motivates mountaineers themselves.

G Today, with a modest technical ability, climbing the mountain is achievable.

Part 7

You are going to read an article about coping with life's problems. For questions **13–22**, choose from the sections (**A–D**). The sections may be chosen more than once.

Mark your answers **on the separate answer sheet**.

Which section

advises against a modern way of doing something?	13
says we should imagine a different outcome to a situation?	14
talks about fear of the unknown?	15
tells us that we can learn from the past?	16
approves of both a modern and old-fashioned way of doing the same thing?	17
focuses on the importance of establishing a routine?	18
suggests following someone else's example?	19
encourages us to plan ahead?	20
reminds us to use an ability we have already developed?	21
mentions an activity that has more than one positive effect on us?	22

Dealing with life's problems!

A Running

Most of us are aware of the physical benefits of running, but equally as important for our well-being are the mental effects – increased clarity of thought, stress relief, etc. When we are running, endorphins are released which give our spirits a definite lift and send the blood to the brain which makes it easier to think clearly. How to run well, though? A good tip is to watch an eight-year-old girl running. Running robotically on a treadmill with a blasting MP3 player, as so many of us do today, is not going to get those happy hormones buzzing. Learn from the child – the steps are springy, the foot gets off the floor quickly and comes down lightly. Tune in to your feet and not the MP3 player.

B Sleeping

Concern about how much sleep we get and worry about all the things we have to do can only increase our problems. If you are a worrier, you will worry and this affects your sleep. So, stick to the ground rules: go to bed and get up at the same time every day, and allow some time to wind down before bed. As for your worries, assign yourself a 'worry period'. This should be in the same place, at the same time every day. Give yourself 15–20 minutes to write down and contemplate a to-do list. And if you're worrying about worrying keeping you awake, remind yourself that your body actually needs less sleep than you think. Although we're told to get eight hours – six to seven hours is absolutely fine.

C Dealing with change

Most of us when faced with change instinctively react by wanting to hold onto things as they are. But you're better at coping with change than you think. In fact, you will already have coped with lots of it in your life and have masses of experience to draw on. So, next time you're faced with a change that feels terrifying, do this: write down all the changes you have experienced at different times in your life. For example, you might have changed school, had a new baby in the family or moved home and so on. Underneath, write down the coping strategies you had to learn in each of these change situations. The point is that those valuable life skills helped you once and will do so again, if you can just remember them and remove some of the inevitable fear that accompanies change.

D Putting it on paper

Sometimes we get stressed about things that have happened and we just think about them over and over again. What if I'd said …? Why didn't he …? Writing down the things that are worrying us or have made us angry can be very therapeutic. It is a way of setting a thought free. Once it's on the page – or screen – we can read it, reread it, delete it or reflect upon it. Writing allows us to access the logical and creative parts of the brain as we connect meaning together. Try it: take something that has bothered you – this could be a conversation or argument which didn't turn out the way you wanted – and write what you wish you'd said or the words of sympathy you wish you'd been offered. Writing a blog may have overtaken diaries, but they are both a means of presenting your thoughts. The style doesn't need to be of a prize-winning standard to have value! It's also something you can look back on in years to come!

Paper 2 Writing

Part 1

You **must** answer this question. Write your answer in **140–190 words** in an appropriate style.

1   You have recently had a discussion in class about choosing a career. Now your teacher has asked you to write an essay.

Write an essay using all the notes and give reasons for your point of view.

Essay question:

Life is much better today than before because of the internet. Do you agree?

Notes:

Things to write about:

1   communication

2   information

3   your own idea

Write your **essay**. You must use grammatically correct sentences with accurate spelling and punctuation in a style appropriate for the situation.

Part 2

Write an answer to **one** of the questions **2–4** in this part. Write your answer in **140–190 words** in an appropriate style.

2   You have received an email from your Australian friend, Kate, who has been invited to a wedding in your country. Read this part of the email and write your email to Kate.

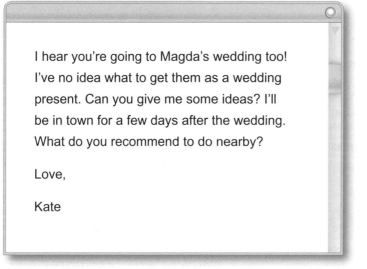

I hear you're going to Magda's wedding too! I've no idea what to get them as a wedding present. Can you give me some ideas? I'll be in town for a few days after the wedding. What do you recommend to do nearby?

Love,

Kate

Write your **email**.

3   An international magazine wants to publish reviews of recent films in its next issue.
Write a review of a film you have seen recently to send to the magazine.

Write your **review**.

4   You have seen the following announcement on a school noticeboard.

> Do you have a favourite spot where you like to chill out? Maybe you read there or listen to music. We are looking for articles with the title 'My Favourite Spot' to include in the school magazine. Send us your article and you might win a prize!

Write your **article**.

Paper 3 Listening

Part 1 ▶ 26

You will hear people talking in eight different situations. For questions **1–8**, choose the best answer (**A**, **B** or **C**).

1 You hear a boy talking about a recent flight he has been on.
   What spoiled the experience for him?
   A his fear of the take-off
   B the length of the journey
   C a delay caused by the weather

2 You hear a phone message about a meeting.
   What does the woman want to do?
   A suggest rearranging their meeting
   B explain why she missed the meeting
   C postpone the meeting until later in the day

3 You hear part of a radio interview with an actress about a recent performance.
   Why did the actress take the role?
   A it was a challenge
   B she hadn't done a Shakespeare play before
   C she wanted to work with a particular director

4 You hear a swimmer talking on radio about a recent race.
   Why did he make a false start?
   A He was badly prepared.
   B He was confused.
   C He was nervous.

5 You hear two friends talking about the sales.
   What advice does the girl give the boy?
   A not to go by car
   B not to get there too early
   C not to expect good bargains

6 You hear a boy and a girl talking about a recent TV programme.
   What did they dislike about the programme?
   A it was too old-fashioned
   B it wasn't true to the book
   C the main actor wasn't right for the part

7 You hear part of a radio news programme.
   What does the presenter say about the severe weather conditions?
   A They caused a short interruption in power supplies.
   B They came as a surprise to many people.
   C They are expected to continue.

8 You hear a boy and a girl talking about a new laptop.
   What is the boy unhappy with?
   A the after sales service
   B the speed of the internet
   C the size and weight

Part 2 ▶ 27

You will hear a girl called Samantha talking to her class about a wedding she attended. For questions **9–18**, complete the sentences.

A wedding in Paris

Samantha says her [____ **9**] was unable to attend the wedding in Paris.

Samantha was upset that the hotel didn't have a [____ **10**] to sit on.

Samantha was annoyed that she'd forgotten to pack the [____ **11**] she wanted to wear for the wedding.

The [____ **12**] in the Town Hall particularly impressed Samantha.

Samantha liked the fact that a [____ **13**] took pictures of the bride and groom.

The city tour was exciting for Samantha because of her interest in [____ **14**] .

Samantha uses the word [____ **15**] to describe the setting for the wedding reception.

Samantha ate a specially prepared [____ **16**] meal at the wedding meal.

There were no [____ **17**] at the wedding, to Samantha's surprise.

The DJ played a song called [____ **18**] , which Samantha liked very much.

Part 3 ▶ 28

You will hear five different people talking about writers they like. For questions **19–23** choose from the list (**A–H**) what motivated each speaker to start reading the writer's books. Use the letters only once. There are three extra letters which you do not need to use.

A	a film adaptation of one of the books	
B	educational requirements	
C	a personal recommendation	Speaker 1 [**19**]
D	a desire to be up-to-date with modern writers	Speaker 2 [**20**]
E	a doctor's advice	Speaker 3 [**21**]
F	a coincidence	Speaker 4 [**22**]
G	a combination of factors	Speaker 5 [**23**]
H	a TV review	

Part 4 ▶ 29

You will hear an interview with a teacher of an exercise form called Zumba. For questions **24–30**, choose the best answer (**A**, **B** or **C**).

24 Vicky decided to become a Zumba instructor when she
  A was praised for her technique.
  B attended a session with a friend.
  C became unemployed.

25 What does Vicky say when asked about the popularity of Zumba?
  A She is surprised that so many people are interested in it.
  B She wondered whether people would take it seriously as a way to keep fit.
  C She thinks people have become bored with other types of exercise.

26 Vicky thinks that people enjoy Zumba because
  A it doesn't require much effort to get right.
  B it's a good way to meet other people.
  C it can be done individually at home.

27 Vicky thinks that to become good at Zumba, you need
  A a basic sense of rhythm.
  B an ability to learn a variety of steps.
  C a certain amount of flexibility.

28 What does Vicky enjoy so much about teaching Zumba?
  A choosing the music she plays while the class works out
  B inventing new steps for her class to try out
  C seeing people become more energetic

29 Vicky says that an unexpected benefit of Zumba includes
  A making the body stronger.
  B increased coordination for everyday tasks.
  C feeling emotionally happier.

30 What is Vicky going to do next?
  A film an exercise video
  B teach a new form of Zumba
  C start up a children's class

Paper 4 Speaking

Part 1

The Interlocutor will ask you and the other candidate some questions about yourselves.

▶ 30 Listen to the recording and answer the questions. Pause the recording after each bleep and give your answer.

Part 2

The Interlocutor will ask you and the other candidate to talk on your own about some photographs.

▶ 31 Listen to the recording and answer the questions. When you hear two bleeps, pause the recording for one minute and answer the question. Then start the recording again. When you hear one bleep, pause the recording for 20 seconds and answer the question.

Candidate A

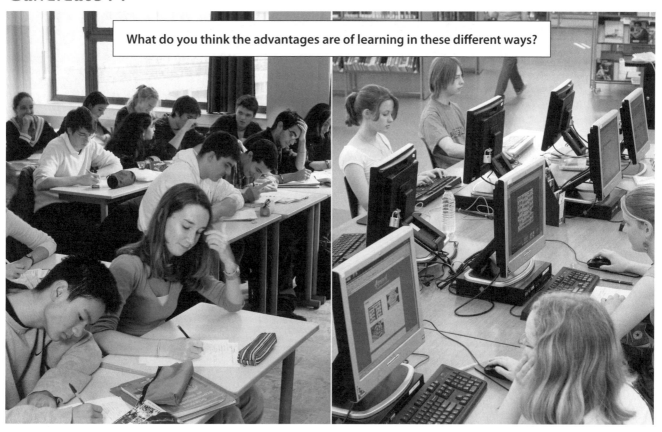

What do you think the advantages are of learning in these different ways?

Candidate B

How do you think the people are feeling?

Part 3

The Interlocutor will ask you and the other candidate to discuss something together.

▶ 32 **Listen to the Interlocutor's instructions and read the options. When you hear the bleep, pause the recording for two minutes and complete the task.**

Listen to the next instruction. When you hear the bleep, pause the recording for one minute and complete the task.

You now have a minute to decide which you think is the most important change and why.

Part 4

The Interlocutor will ask you and the other candidate questions related to the topic of Part 3.

▶ 33 **Listen to the recording and answer the Interlocutor's questions. Pause the recording when you hear each bleep and discuss the question with the other candidate.**

Answer key

UNIT 1

Listening

1 1 B 2 C 3 A 4 B

Vocabulary

1 1 get 2 to 3 chat 4 send 5 lose 6 download 7 catch 8 keep

Grammar

1 1 I **am not going** to the school reunion next month. 2 Shh! I**'m speaking** to your aunt on the phone. 3 Tara **is having** a hard time trying to get the phone company to replace her mobile. 4 I **find** it easy to misunderstand what people mean in text messages. 5 Miguel **is** a real whizz on the computer – he can do anything! 6 Jenny's flight **leaves** at three o'clock. She's going to visit her cousin in Australia. 7 It **is becoming** harder and harder to keep in touch with old friends. 8 I**'m visiting** my cousin in hospital tonight.

2 Hi, Suzana!
I **(1) am looking forward to** the school reunion next week! **(2) Are you coming?** I hope so! I'm so happy that our old school **(3) is organising** such an exciting event. I **(4) remember** so much about our school days! I **(5) am** out of touch with some of our old friends now, so I can't wait to talk to everyone face to face about what they **(6) are doing** these days.
The party **(7) starts** at seven o'clock, so if you like, I can pick you up after I **(8) finish** work at six. Let me know!
Love,
Zena

3 1 look forward to (state/action) 2 come (action) 3 organise (action) 4 remember (state) 5 be (state) 6 do (action) 7 start (action) 8 finish (action)

4 State verbs: depend, hear, like, own, smell

Use of English

1 1 B 2 A 3 D 4 C 5 D 6 A 7 A 8 B

Reading

1 A holiday rep is the person who represents the holiday company and makes sure that the customers enjoy their holiday.

3 1 impatient people or people who like regular working hours 2 at least eighteen 3 French and Spanish 4 newspapers, travel magazines, the internet 5 accommodation and a uniform 6 swimming pool, tennis courts

4 1 A 2 A 3 B 4 A 5 B 6 A
5 1 B 2 A 3 A 4 B 5 A 6 B

Grammar

1 Hi, Andrei!
I'm here on holiday in Hungary with my family – my grandparents are Hungarian, so it's great to be with people who know the country really well. We're staying in a cottage in the countryside and there's a lake nearby where we enjoy **(1) swimming** every morning. I'd love **(2) to do** this at home too, but there's nowhere fun to go.
I'm also learning **(3) to fish**! I'm not usually keen on fishing but my granddad makes it great fun.
(4) Spending all day in the sun is pretty tiring, so before we have dinner we take a short nap. I like **(5) eating** outdoors – the food definitely tastes better! I'm looking forward to **(6) seeing** you. Let's **(7) see** that new action film when I get back.
I'd better **(8) go** now. See you soon!
Pete

2 1 We'd better not ~~to~~ be late home from school – we're visiting Grandma this evening.
2 I'd love **to** go to Kenya on holiday. I've never been to Africa.
3 I can't wait **to** get my new phone – it's got some fantastic apps!
4 Let's ~~to~~ buy a present for Dad's birthday. What do you think he would like?
5 Stephanie's hoping **to** pass her Travel and Tourism exam. She worked really hard.
6 Jo's learning **to** be a tour guide. He wants to work in Spain.
7 I've arranged **to** have a new website built for my work.
8 You should ~~to~~ check your passport is valid before you travel.

Speaking

1 1 B 2 A 3 D 4 no answer 5 H 6 C 7 G 8 no answer 9 E 10 F

Writing

1 1 so 2 think 3 reason 4 Because 5 However 6 mean 7 true 8 For 9 matter

2 are the oldest friends really the best?
They have shared important experiences with you
For me, the best friends are the ones you can rely on

3 1 D 2 E 3 F 4 A 5 C 6 B

4 Sample answer:

When we have a problem or need to make an important decision, it's really good to have people around you who can give you good advice. But is it better to ask someone in your family or one of your friends?

In my opinion it depends a lot on what the problem or decision is about. For example, if you need advice about money or work, then maybe it's good to ask someone in the family. Alternatively, if it's a personal problem, like dealing with a boyfriend or girlfriend, your friends might be better.

Obviously, the relationship you have with your family and friends is an important factor too. Some people don't get on well with their family, so asking for advice might not be a good idea! Also, sometimes your friends know you even better than your family does.

In addition to this, it's important to remember that for some advice we need to speak to someone completely different, like a teacher or a doctor. All problems are different. The important thing is that people mustn't be afraid of asking for advice – whoever they choose to ask.

UNIT 2

Vocabulary

1 1 surprised 2 confused 3 annoyed
4 exhausting 5 amusing 6 upset

2 1 fascinating 2 worried 3 embarrassed
4 scared 5 thrilled 6 depressed

3 fascinating, thrilled

Speaking

1 1 changed their appearance 2 have chosen

2 1 Both 2 in 3 whereas 4 might 5 So
6 excited 7 however 8 look

Listening

1 1 two 2 Suzy 3 she won the lottery

2 1 a place 2 a feeling 3 an object
4 a place/object 5 an object 6 a country

3 1 bookshop 2 worried 3 watch 4 library
5 camera 6 Spain

Vocabulary

1 1 C 2 A 3 C 4 B 5 B 6 B 7 C 8 C

Grammar

1 1 A 2 F 3 D 4 B 5 E 6 C

2 1 I've been **went** to London on a business trip last week.
2 Life **has changed** over the last few years for animals that live in the Polar Regions.
3 I did wear **wore** cool clothes when I was a teenager.
4 Megan has **got up** early this morning and did her homework before lunch.
5 The town I live in grew **has grown** a lot since I've lived here.
6 People became **have become** more and more conscious of the need for responsible tourism.
7 Gina has **bought** some new glasses at the weekend. They look great!
8 The invention of the wheel has **changed** the world forever.

Reading

1 C

2 1 (travel) article
2 the travel article (*10 wonders of the disappearing world*)
3 the travel article
4 threatened places

3 1 C 2 F 3 B 4 A 5 E

4 1 glee 2 destination 3 fragile 4 threatened
5 damaging 6 powerful

Grammar

1 1 When I was a child I **used to** have blond hair but now it's dark brown.
2 Tommy **went** to Rome last week on holiday. Lucky him!
3 I **used to** love sitting by the fire listening to my grandma telling stories.
4 Michaela **said** she enjoyed the party on Saturday.
5 Tina **sent** Angelo a text to arrange a time to meet last night.
6 On Saturday, Grace and Joe **had** a meal in a restaurant and then saw a film.

2 What did you **(1) use to** want to be when you were a kid? I wanted to be a professional footballer. Even when I was really little, I **(2) used to/would** spend hours kicking a ball around in the street where I lived. I **(3) didn't use to** have the best football or the smartest trainers but I had so much energy and passion for the sport. My mum **(4) used to/would** have to come and find me at mealtimes – I didn't hear her calling because I was so absorbed in my practice! I **(5) used to/would** watch every match on TV and I **(6) used to** know the names of all the footballers. Sometimes, my dad **(7) used to/would** take me to watch a live match and I loved it! I **(8) used to** have a really powerful kick but then I got injured and that was the end of my dreams of becoming a professional player. I still watch my team but I don't play anymore. I'm more into music these days and now I want to be a rock star!

Use of English

1 How using the internet has changed the way students do homework.

2 Linking words: than (part of the phrase 'rather than'), While
Verbs: are (auxiliary verb), have (auxiliary verb), make (part of collocation 'make sure')
Pronouns: them
Prepositions: out (part of phrasal verb 'run out of')
Articles: the

3 **1** While **2** than **3** are **4** out **5** make **6** have **7** them **8** the

Writing

1 **1** let **2** as **3** went **4** guess **5** absolutely **6** tells **7** news **8** Lots

2 1, 4, 6, 8

3 **Sample answer:**
Hi Max,

How kind of your parents! You're going to have a fantastic time. I absolutely love decorating. I did my room last year, but I get bored quickly so I'd love to do it again.

You know, I think a room tells you a lot about the owner's personality. So, for your room, I think you should go for pale colours, maybe white, pale blues and browns – nothing too bright. Also, bright colours aren't that relaxing in a bedroom, are they? And I know you like to spend time in your room reading and painting. Some of your paintings would look lovely on pale walls.

Regarding furniture – how about getting a really big, old-style bed? Your room is big and your house is lovely and old. I think it would look great. I'd take up the carpet too and have some bright rugs. Oh, yes and lamps instead of a central light.

Have fun and send me a photo!

Hope to see you soon,
Love
Jenny

UNIT 3

Listening

1 **A** 4 **B** 3 **C** 1 **D** 2

2 **1** E **2** C **3** A **4** B

Vocabulary

1 **1** was tough at **2** passionate about
3 I stuck with it **4** takes/can take a lifetime
5 got hooked on computer games

2 **1** do **2** went **3** playing **4** do **5** plays **6** do **7** going **8** doing

3 **1** in **2** about **3** at **4** about **5** at/in **6** by **7** at **8** into

Grammar

1 Countable: (1) languages, (2) skills, (6) people, (8) children
Uncountable: (3) money, (4) work, (5) experience, (7) knowledge

2 Abstract: love, news, , skills, values
Concrete: bread, oil, pasta, silver

3 **1** Caroline has learned a great new recipe for **pasta** and sauce in her Italian cooking class.
2 I've learned how to top up my car with **oil** in the car maintenance workshop.
3 Steve listens to the **news** every day – he likes to know what's happening in the world.
4 I've baked **bread** to eat with the soup. I hope you like it!
5 Zeke's into making jewellery from **silver** for men.
6 Doing an evening class is a great way to develop new **skills**.
7 Your **values** are the things you believe in.
8 Dina and Ned share a **love** of playing sport.

4 **1** There's **a** fashion design course you might be interested in at my college. I'll give you **some/a lot of/lots of** information about it next time I see you.
2 Chris, can you add milk to the shopping list? There isn't **any/much/a lot** left. We need **some** biscuits, too. Oh, and can you get **some** oranges?
3 There's only **a little** coffee in the jar – would you like tea instead?
4 Jen, do you have **any/some** guitar music I could borrow? I really want to learn to play.
5 **Few** children seem to enjoy playing outside these days. It's a pity.
6 How **many** people were at the pool today? There weren't **many** when I went the other day.

5 **1** I don't have ~~many~~ **much/any** interest in sport, I'm afraid.
2 How ~~much~~ **many** times have you run a marathon?
3 There ~~are~~ **is** lots of cheese in the fridge if you fancy a snack.
4 Do you have **any** albums by Justin Bieber? He's so cool.
5 I love listening to **a little** classical music to relax.
6 I've got **a lot of/lots of** hobbies and I'm always busy at the weekends.

Speaking

1   **1** F   **2** T   **3** F   **4** F   **5** T   **6** T

2   **1** A   **2** D   **3** E   **4** C   **5** B

3   **1** Let's   **2** about   **3** In   **4** agree   **5** on   **6** think
    7 point   **8** What   **9** For   **10** choose

4   Organising the discussion:
    Let's begin with …
    Let's move on.
    So, that's the one we choose?
    Involving your partner:
      What about picture 2?
      Do you agree?
      Don't you think?
      What do you think … ?
    Giving an opinion:
      In my opinion …
      That's a good point.
      For me, it's the TV show.

Reading

1   A

2   **1** B   **2** A   **3** B   **4** C   **5** B   **6** C

3   **1** picked up   **2** let down   **3** go ahead
    4 ended up   **5** set out   **6** gave up

Grammar

1   **1** I**'ve been counting** up the money we raised for
      charity. I'll carry on after lunch.
    2 Have you ever **tried** gardening? It's not as boring as
      people think.
    3 Sue **has been training** for the marathon for weeks.
    4 I**'ve been ringing** Maria all afternoon. I think she's at
      the gym.

2   I'm passionate about rhythm and I **(1) 've always been**
into dance forms that are percussive – in other words,
where you make a noise on the floor with your feet! I
(2) 've been doing tap dance classes since I was ten
and more recently I **(3) 've taken up** clog dancing – a
traditional form of dance that, where I come from,
(4) grew up in factories in the late 1800s. The story
goes that factory workers, who **(5) wore** wooden
shoes for work, started dancing in them and imitated
the sounds that the factory machines made.
In fact, clog dancing **(6) has probably been** around
for hundreds of years and over the last decade or so,
it **(7) has been making** a comeback in the UK. There
are festivals all over the country and my dance group
(8) has just raised over £1,000 for charity by doing a
'dance-a-thon', where we danced non-stop for twelve
hours! Since then, we **(9) 've been working** really hard
on a new dance routine and we're going to enter a
competition. We'll be on stage in front of hundreds of
people – I **(10) 've never felt** so nervous! It'll be great
fun, though.

Use of English

1   **1** D   **2** F   **3** B   **4** A   **5** E   **6** C

2   **1** unusual   **2** competitions   **3** famous   **4** excited
    5 hopeless   **6** comfortable   **7** creative
    8 children

Writing

1   **1** ever   **2** came   **3** awards   **4** follows
    5 remarkable   **6** combines   **7** found   **8** seem

2   **Sample answer:**
    Fearless
I don't usually enjoy documentaries because they can
be a bit boring, but I watched one last weekend which
I thought was really excellent.

It was called *Fearless!* and it follows people who do
extreme sports. It isn't about bungee jumping or sky
diving or the sports we usually expect to see. It's about
much scarier sports than those! It shows one girl who
skis down mountains very fast – not to get to the
bottom, but straight off the edge of a cliff! She flies
through the air and waits to the last moment before
opening her parachute!

The thing I love about this documentary is the filming.
It is really remarkable and it shows that the film crew
are very brave people too. It also shows us the lives of
some very special people who live for danger.
I found this an absolutely fascinating documentary and
I hope it wins lots of awards because it deserves them.
You must see it if you can!

UNIT 4

Reading

1   **1** C   **2** A   **3** C

2   **1** D   **2** E   **3** A   **4** F   **5** B   **6** C

3   **1** C   **2** B   **3** A   **4** B   **5** C   **6** A

4   **1** lead   **2** conduct   **3** on   **4** way   **5** keep
    6 narrow

Grammar

1   **1** F   **2** A   **3** D   **4** C   **5** E   **6** B

2   What a trip I had last month! My friend, Noela,
(1) invited/had invited me to her 21st birthday in
Oporto, Portugal. She studied English with me in
London last summer and we had stayed in touch.
This was a chance to see her again and I **(2) was
looking forward to** it. I **(3) had booked** my flights
and accommodation, found a great outfit to wear and
bought a cool gift for Noela.
On the day of the party, everything was going really
well. I **(4) had arrived** in Oporto the night before,
the weather was beautiful and I was really excited to
be in a city I **(5) had never been** to before. I set off
from my hostel in the direction of the hotel where the

party was taking place. I got onto the tram and **(6) was looking** at the map of the city in my guidebook when I suddenly realised I **(7) was going** in the wrong direction!

I quickly got off the tram and looked around. Then I **(8) realised** I was lost in a strange city without knowing a word of Portuguese! Fortunately, a very kind lady saw me looking at my map and she asked me in English where I wanted to go. I **(9) explained** the situation and then she smiled and pointed across the road. I **(10) was standing** opposite the hotel! I had been going in the right direction after all!

3
1 *Afterwards/As soon as/When* I reached the hotel, I went for a swim in the pool.
2 *While/When/As soon as* Sue had booked the travel arrangements, she rang to tell me.
3 Michael cooked dinner for Petra *after/when/by the time* she got home from her trip.
4 *While/During/After* the sun was going down, we sipped cocktails on the balcony.
5 I was really hungry *by the time/afterwards/when* I had finished skiing.
6 *During/While/When* Jay was collecting the luggage, he dropped a suitcase on his toe.
7 The flight was so tiring that *as soon as/by the time/when* I got home, I went to bed and slept for twelve hours.
8 *During/When/While* my trip to Morocco I went to see the city of Casablanca.

Speaking

1
1 probably   2 imagine   3 if   4 might   5 looks
6 sure

2
1 C   2 B   3 A

Listening

1
1 *Who would believe it?*   2 Sweden (north east)
3 He lived.

2
1 A   2 B   3 A   4 C   5 B

Vocabulary

1

T	D	O	D	I	K	V	A	N	N	O	T
S	T	F	R	E	E	Z	I	N	G	C	X
S	E	E	X	H	A	U	S	T	E	D	E
C	J	T	R	T	R	F	P	S	E	K	R
F	Z	S	V	R	I	I	E	P	E	D	D
S	T	A	R	V	I	N	G	N	R	E	B
J	E	J	E	R	D	F	Y	C	I	O	S
T	X	O	F	A	H	J	Y	F	O	N	B
F	A	S	C	I	N	A	T	I	N	G	G
T	E	R	R	I	B	L	E	E	N	A	E
E	N	O	R	M	O	U	S	J	P	G	C
A	X	I	N	U	B	O	I	L	I	N	G

2
1 deafening   2 starving   3 enormous   4 terrifying
5 freezing   6 tiny

Grammar

1
1 A   2 B   3 B   4 A   5 A   6 B

2
1 B   2 D   3 C   4 A   5 F   6 E

Use of English

1
1 looks as if it's   2 has been a pilot for
3 while I was playing   4 was absolutely freezing
5 turned up late so   6 found the exhibition

Writing

1
1, 4, 5, 6

3
A 2   B 4   C 5   D 1   E 6   F 3

4
Sample answer:
Introduction
The aim of this report is to advise students about security and safety at the swimming pool in the leisure building.

Poolside safety
It is important not to run on the poolside as this can be very dangerous. People can trip or fall over easily. Also, students are asked not to dive in the shallow end of the pool. There have been several accidents recently.

Lockers
Lockers with keys are provided in the changing rooms to keep your clothes and possessions safe. Please use them. We recommend leaving any valuable jewellery with the receptionist.

Accidents
If there is an accident in or near the pool, the lifeguard must be informed. He will contact the college nurse or give First Aid. If the fire bell rings, instructions about leaving the building can be found on all doors leading to the pool.

Conclusion
The pool is popular with students and following the advice given should ensure that students can continue to enjoy swimming activities at the college.

UNIT 5

Vocabulary

1

			¹b	r	o	w	s	e
	²b	r	a	n	d			
			³c	r	e	d	i	t
		⁴l	o	g	o			
			⁵m	a	r	k	e	t
	⁶c	e	n	t	r	e		
⁷s	e	c	o	n	d	h	a	n	d

2 **1** centre/mall **2** market **3** bargains **4** browse
5 credit **6** second-hand **7** bargains **8** logo

Listening

1 **1** B **2** D **3** A **4** C **5** E
2 **1** B **2** A **3** A **4** B **5** C

Grammar

1 **1** *I'm taking/I'm going to take/~~I take~~* that new phone
back to the shop this morning – it isn't working
properly.
2 *~~I'll meet~~/I'm meeting/I'm going to meet* Tina at the
leather market at 3 p.m. She wants to buy a new
bag.
3 Where do you think *~~I'm getting~~/I might get/I'll get*
the best deal on a second-hand car?
4 Oh no! The website's crashed on the payments page.
I'll have to/~~I'm having to~~/I'm going to have to start
again!
5 I think *I'll look at/~~I look at~~/I might look at* some of
those price comparison websites for travel insurance
later. It depends how tired I am after work.
6 The bank *~~might close~~/closes/will close* at 4 p.m., so
I'd better go and pay the money in now.

2 Hi, Charlie!
What **(1) are you doing/going to do** this evening? I'm
(2) going to go/going shopping. It's my twin brother
and sister's birthday on Sunday. I've got lots to buy, so
I'm going into town after my classes.
I **(3) 'm going to buy/buying** my sister a voucher and
for my brother, an alarm clock – he loves his gadgets! I
think they'll be really pleased with those.
After shopping, I **(4) 'm meeting** my friends and we
(5) 're going to have dinner at our favourite pizza
restaurant. One of my friends, Steph, hasn't been
before but I'm sure she **(6) 'll like** it. Then we **(7) might
go** to see a late-night film at the cinema which starts
at 11 p.m. but it depends how tired we are!
I **(8) 'll write** again soon.
Love,
Elena

Speaking

1 **1** Let's **2** could **3** about **4** might **5** don't
6 work **7** sure **8** agree
2 **1** That might work **2** I'm not too sure
3 **1** mean **2** right **3** depends **4** would **5** could
6 maybe **7** idea **8** then **9** about **10** not

Reading

1 **2** exchanged
2 **1** E **2** G **3** A **4** C **5** F **6** B
3 **1** odd **2** worthless **3** handy **4** glanced
5 odd jobs **6** irrelevant

Grammar

1 I'm from Spain and I came to live in the UK a few
months ago. I'm a shopaholic and I *love* shopping!
But it's taken me a while to **(1) get used to** shopping
here. I live in a village and the shops close at 5.30 p.m.
I **(2) am not used to** that because in Spain they're
open much later and I **(3) am used to** being able
to go shopping after work. I can't do that now, so I
have to either shop online or wait until the weekend.
One thing I **(4) am not used to** is the prices because
they're much higher in the UK. It's taken me ages to
(5) get used to shopping without comparing how
much I'd spend on a similar item back home. The sizes
are different too, so I can't just walk into a shop and
pick something up without trying it like I **(6) was
used to**!

2 **1** I still haven't got used to ~~get~~ **getting** up so early for
my new job.
2 Sue didn't think she'd like living on her own but she
is used to it now.
3 I got used to ~~do~~ **doing** all my shopping online
when I lived in a small village.
4 Antonio said it is too difficult to ~~be~~ **get** used to the
British weather so he's going back to Portugal.
5 Jen is **not** used to getting so much attention from
the media. It's all new to her and she hates it.
6 It took me ages to ~~be~~ **get** used to living in a big city
but I love it now.

Use of English

1 **1** F **2** C **3** B **4** D **5** A **6** E
2 **1** B **2** C **3** A **4** D **5** A **6** B **7** D **8** D

Writing

1 **1** F **2** F **3** T **4** F **5** F
2 **1** all **2** course **3** well **4** However **5** view
6 balance
3 **1** On balance **2** Of course **3** In my view
4 First of all **5** However **6** As well as this

4 **Sample answer:**

Obviously, having enough money is important for everyone. We need to earn enough to pay for somewhere to live, food, clothes and other necessities and we work hard to do this. If we're lucky, we earn more than we need and we can choose what we do with this. Some people spend the extra; others save it. Which is better?

First of all, I think it's important to enjoy our lives as much as possible. We spend a lot of time working, so we should spend time having fun too. Why not spend money on doing things we enjoy – like going out or buying music?

Some people worry about the future and prefer to save money in case they lose their jobs or get ill. Saving money gives them some security.

Personally, I don't think the answer to the question is either to save or to spend. As far as I'm concerned, we need to do both. We don't know what is going to happen in the future, but also we need to enjoy our lives. So, spend fifty percent and save fifty percent – that's the best answer for me!

UNIT 6

Vocabulary

1 **1** a sense **2** prospects **3** balance **4** well
5 full **6** application
2 **1** C **2** F **3** G **4** E **5** H **6** D **7** A **8** B
3 **1** stressful **2** secure **3** permanent **4** salary
5 rewarding **6** interview

Speaking

1 **1** window cleaning
2 they do not discuss or reach a decision as to which job is most rewarding
2 ✓: 1, 6
3 **1** B **2** E **3** A **4** D **5** C
A That's an interesting **B** It all **C** To be
D I've never thought **E** to think of it

Reading

1 **1** T **2** F
2 **1** C **2** A **3** C **4** B **5** A **6** B **7** C
8 A **9** B **10** A
3 **1** struggle **2** decent **3** response **4** try out
5 was hooked **6** expert

Grammar

1 **1** Sheila works **slower** than Lin but her work is more accurate.
2 Andula is a tree surgeon. She says it's the **most dangerous** job she's ever had.
3 Charlie works the **longest** hours of anyone I know.
4 Theresa has been much **happier** since she got a promotion.
5 Steven's job is much **better** paid than mine.
6 Now that I've moved house, I don't have as far to travel to work **as** I used to.
2 **1** No one in the department is as **good as** Megan at computer programming.
2 This is **the most impressive** application letter I've ever read.
3 Jean **is less experienced** than Rob in managing people.
4 The new machinery is **(much) more efficient than** the old machinery.
5 He's a **much fairer boss than** any other I've had.
6 This is **the worst job** I've ever had.
3 **A:** How are you enjoying your new job, Chris?
B: t's great, thanks. A lot of the people in my department are **(1) older than** me and have worked for the company for a long time. They're **(2) more experienced than** me, which is good because I'm learning a lot from them. I'm starting to feel **(3) more confident** in my role now.
A: That's good. Are your presentation skills improving, too?
B: Yes! I gave my first presentation to new clients last week. It was **(4) the biggest** group of people I've ever spoken to and it went really well.

Use of English

1 voluntary work experience
2 **1** to **2** which/that **3** with **4** because/as
5 had **6** are **7** of **8** when/after

Listening

1 **1** F **2** T
2 **1** romantic **2** comedies **3** (karate) teacher
4 climbing **5** (stunt) degree **6** shopping
7 height **8** statue

Grammar

1 **1** I **don't have to** wear a uniform for my job. It's great because I can wear my jeans to work if I want to!
2 Peter **had to** leave home very early to get the train to work. He had a meeting at 7.00 a.m.!
3 We **were supposed to** move to the new offices today but they still aren't ready.
4 You **don't need to** switch the computers off – I'll do it before I leave.
5 You **should** ask for a pay rise. Your salary hasn't increased for three years.
6 You **mustn't** handle food without washing your hands first because they could be dirty.

2 This is a fantastic opportunity for the right person. Yummy Chocs Ltd require an in-store market researcher to collect customer feedback on samples of our premier chocolate ranges. Here's what the role involves:

Placed in a variety of stores across the North West, you will meet customers on a daily basis, so you will **(1) have to/need to** dress smartly at all times.

Talking to customers about their tastes is an essential part of this role, so you **(2) have to/need to/must** be a friendly and sociable person.

You will be part of a team of co-workers who will get together regularly to discuss and analyse customer feedback. Therefore you **(3) have to/need to/must** enjoy working with others to share your ideas.

You don't **(4) have to/need to** have a qualification in food science or marketing but you **(5) have to/need to/must** be passionate about chocolate.

You **(6) don't have to/don't need to** send proof of qualifications at this point but if you think you've got what it takes, send your CV and covering letter to the address below.

Writing

1 Doesn't say when available for interview

2 **1** Hi, Mrs Randall   **2** I want to apply
3 What's the pay and what are the hours?
4 Please write soon

3 **Sample answer:**
Dear Mr. Deacon,

I saw your advertisement in the Daily Echo on Thursday and I should like to apply for a job helping with make-up for the film *Robin Hood*.

I am currently following a film and theatre course at Southway College and I am particularly interested in make-up for film. I have helped with the make-up for several short films that our college students have made and I attach some references from my college tutors.

I finish my second year studies at the end of June and I shall then be free until college starts again on October 4th.

If you think I might be suitable to work on the film, please contact me at the above address. I am available to come for interview any Wednesday. I should also be grateful if you could send me further details about dates and payment.

Yours sincerely,
Patrick Kyle

UNIT 7

Speaking

1 Student A: 1, 4, 6
Student B: 5

2 **1** Both   **2** look   **3** probably   **4** imagine   **5** might
6 definitely   **7** other   **8** seem   **9** sure   **10** must

Use of English

1 **1** unfriendly   **2** impatient   **3** disloyal
4 irresponsible   **5** unlucky   **6** incomplete

2 **1** helpful   **2** thoughtless   **3** powerful   **4** harmless
5 useful   **6** colourful

3 **1** unexpected   **2** hopeful   **3** impossible
4 satisfaction   **5** Activities   **6** effective
7 musical   **8** ability

Vocabulary

1

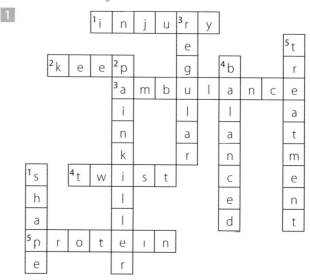

2 **1** protein   **2** twisted   **3** shape   **4** keep
5 injury   **6** balanced

3 **1** benefits   **2** down   **3** aching   **4** balanced
5 catch   **6** out   **7** expectancy   **8** blocked
9 picked   **10** medicine

Grammar

1   Tina123, 1/08/12, 8.14 a.m.

I watched this fascinating programme last night about exercise. It said that if you did just three minutes of intense exercise a week, you **(1) would get** huge health benefits! Experts reckon that natural, everyday movement could be better for us than doing regular workout sessions at the gym. Apparently, doing quick bursts of exercise, where you run or cycle as hard as you can for less than a minute each time, keeps you fit. They said that if you exercise like this, it **(2) keeps** you in shape, but it also makes you want to eat less – whereas exercising for longer periods makes you hungrier! Cool!

BusyBea, 01/08/12, 9.41 a.m.

I **(3) will be** really annoyed if they find out this is true because I'm a personal trainer and my job depends on people employing me to help them do training workouts. I wouldn't get paid much if I only **(4) worked** for three minutes with each customer!

Gino, 01/08/12, 2.03 p.m.

Well, I guess if you **(5) are** a lazy person, this way of exercising sounds like a great idea. But just three minutes of exercise a week?! That's ridiculous.

ZigZagZoo, 02/08/12, 1.31 a.m.

I work really long hours and don't have time to go to the gym. So, if this worked, I **(6) would find** time to try it.

DanDan, 03/08/12, 6.15 p.m.

If you **(7) don't exercise** you get fat and that's a fact. But only doing three minutes a week? Doesn't sound enough to me.

FunnyMouse, 03/08/12, 10.42 p.m.

Think of all the time you **(8) would save** if this was true! Instead of being bored at the gym or jogging round the streets when it's dark in winter, you could be doing something much more interesting, like seeing friends or going to the cinema. Great idea!

2   **1** If I'm hungry, I eat eggs because they fill me up.
 2 What would you do if you twisted your ankle?
 3 I would take a painkiller if I had a headache.
 4 I'll give you that diet information if you want it.
 5 If I were you, I would go to bed earlier.
 6 Do you drink milk if your muscles ache after exercise/after exercise if your muscles ache?

Listening

1   Speaker 1 – C
 Speaker 2 – D
 Speaker 3 – B
 Speaker 4 – A

2   **1** E   **2** C   **3** B   **4** A

Grammar

1   **1** ~~Provided that~~ **Unless** this cough clears up soon, I'll go to the doctor's for a prescription.
 2 I must stop eating so much, ~~provided that~~ **otherwise** I'll get fat.
 3 You'll have health problems ~~otherwise~~ **unless** you eat healthily and take regular exercise.
 4 Steve wants to be a nurse ~~unless~~ **provided that** he passes his final exams.
 5 If you want, I'll give you a lift to the hospital. ~~Unless~~ **Otherwise** I'll see you later instead.
 6 Jenny said she would help me with my exercise plan this week ~~unless~~ **provided that** she has the time.

2   Open any health magazine and you'll see hundreds of adverts for vitamins and minerals. I've tried many of them, but I haven't noticed any real differences in my health. In fact, I think that **(1) unless** you have a particularly poor diet, you should get everything you need from what you eat. But am I right about this? I asked health expert Brian Peacock for advice. 'Yes, you're right,' he tells me. '**(2) Provided that** you stick to a healthy eating plan, you shouldn't need to take additional vitamins or minerals. **(3) Unless** your body is suffering from a lack of a particular vitamin and your doctor gives you a prescription for something, you should be fine – **(4) otherwise** you could be taking more vitamins than your body actually needs.' He goes on to tell me that beliefs have changed in the medical profession over the benefits of taking extra vitamins and minerals. '**(5) Unless** you're pregnant, when taking folic acid is recommended, don't bother wasting your money. Buying vitamins from health food shops is expensive, so **(6) unless** you've been specifically advised to take them, leave them on the shelf.'

Reading

2   **1** A   **2** C   **3** C   **4** B   **5** A   **6** B

3   **1** to   **2** to   **3** on   **4** from   **5** in   **6** to   **7** with   **8** to

Writing

1   Help! Any ideas?   Love,

2   2, 5, 7

3   **1** hear   **2** sorry   **3** well   **4** idea   **5** don't   **6** about

3 Sample answer:

Hi Pia,

Thanks for your email. It was lovely to hear from you!

I'm really enjoying life at my new school. I've made some great friends and the teachers are nice too. Of course, I miss everyone at my old school but I'm sure we'll all keep in touch.

It's good to hear that you're still doing well at swimming and congratulations on winning last week! One day you'll be in the Olympics! Do you still have to get up at five o'clock for early morning training?

I'm sorry to hear that you're not sleeping. That can be so horrible! But it's quite normal. I don't sleep before exams because I worry so much! Why don't you try drinking some hot milk before you go to bed? Or, how about having a nice warm bath? That always makes me sleepy.

Anyway, I hope all goes well with the competition. Don't worry – you'll be fine! Do let me know how you get on.

Thinking of you,
Love,
Kate

UNIT 8

Vocabulary

1 **1** cat **2** wings **3** fish **4** bear **5** snake
2 **1** F **2** F **3** F **4** T **5** F **6** F **7** T **8** F **9** T
10 F

Listening

1 **1** Michelle is a 17-year old girl with sight problems.
2 Rufus is her guide dog.
2 **1** A **2** B **3** C **4** A **5** C **6** A
3 **1** M **2** R **3** R **4** M **5** R **6** M

Grammar

1 **1** Zoo animals **are looked after** very well these days.
2 My dog, Zack, **is being seen** by the vet at the moment.
3 The kitten **was rescued** by the fire service when he got stuck up a tree.
4 The fences **were repaired** at the safari park because a small animal escaped!
5 I've just had a call from the stables to say my horse **has been stolen**! I can't believe that's happened.
6 The animal rescue centre **has been given** a large donation by the local government.

2 Rudyard Kipling was a British author who wrote a series of stories for children called the *Just So Stories*. These fabulous tales are a work of fantasy, in which strange things happen to animals and people. They **(1) were first published** in 1902 and they describe how animals – in the writer's imagination – **(2) have changed/changed** from their original form to how they appear today. Some changes **(3) were made** by humans, while others happened magically.

In *How the camel got his hump*, the camel **(4) was given** the hump on his back as a punishment for refusing to work and in *The sing-song of Old Man Kangaroo*, we find out how the kangaroo got his powerful back legs from **(5) being chased** by a wild dog all day. The dog **(6) was sent** to chase the kangaroo after the kangaroo **(7) (had) asked** to be made different from all other animals. The original editions of the stories **(8) were illustrated** by the author himself and they **(9) are still enjoyed** by children and adults today. Editions of the stories **(10) have also been released** on DVD, so that people can watch them too.

Speaking

1 **1** people **2** how **3** important
2 **1** say **2** right **3** mean **4** know **5** mean
6 understand **7** saying **8** again
3 **1** C **2** D **3** A **4** E **5** B

Reading

1 He learned about family relationships, love and respect.
2 **1** B **2** G **3** C **4** F **5** E **6** A
3 **1** tough **2** smashed **3** turning point **4** respect
5 astounding **6** beg

Grammar

1 **1** We **have had our garden made** into a habitat for butterflies.
2 We **have had our old windows replaced** with double glazing.
3 We **had a solar panel installed** on our roof.
4 We **had some curtains fitted** that keep in the heat.
5 We**'re going to have some of our lawn made** into a vegetable patch.
6 We **had our coal fire replaced** with a wood burner.

Use of English

1 **1** after **2** of **3** of **4** on **5** about **6** for **7** of
8 with

2 **1** had his car washed
2 do it/break the window on purpose
3 was caused/done by the hurricane
4 has filled up
5 have been changes
6 whether it's/it is a
7 need to find
8 can be reduced

Writing

1 1, 3

2 **1** the red squirrel
2 because of competition from the grey squirrel
3 The writer loves the red squirrels and thinks it is a shame they are disappearing.

3 **1** sadly, unfortunately **2** pretty, clever, beautiful, native **3** clever, big, strong, unwanted
4 dying out/pushing out **5** survive **6** hunt
7 habitat **8** invader

4 **1** no, this is dull
2 no, this is too factual/unengaging
3 no, a direct question is more engaging
4 no, the colloquial tone used in the article works well

5 Sample answer:
__Where have they gone?__
When we talk about 'endangered animals', we usually think of big, beautiful animals like the polar bear or the eagle. However, in my country, there is a very small animal that is definitely under threat but no one talks about it much. It's a lovely animal that we often used to see in our gardens. Many people know it from children's stories too. It's the hedgehog!

What's happening to hedgehogs? Apparently, these amazing little animals are having lots of problems these days. This is for several reasons. One is that we are building lots of new roads. Hedgehogs often travel a couple of miles every night to find food and they use traditional routes, but cars on the new roads are killing them. Also, their habitats are disappearing. There aren't so many bushes and fields near the towns as there used to be. Another reason is changes to our climate which are killing insects that the hedgehogs usually eat.

Sadly, hedgehogs are slowly disappearing. If we don't help them, there won't be any left by the year 2020. That would be a terrible shame, wouldn't it?

UNIT 9

Listening

1 **1** She is talking to her classmates.
2 She has designed a house for the future.

2 **1** weather **2** recycling **3** packaging
4 sleeping bag **5** bathroom **6** voice
7 microwave **8** dish **9** fridge **10** helmet

Vocabulary

1 **1** monitor **2** keyboards **3** software **4** avatar
5 passwords **6** attached

2 **1** save, lose **2** Click, bring **3** Scroll
4 Log, entering **5** Download, print **6** crashes

Grammar

1 **1** There's no way we**'ll be living** on the moon any time soon.
2 I'm so pleased John **will have made** dinner by the time I get home. He said it will on the table waiting, so I won't have to cook.
3 At this time tomorrow I**'ll be swimming** in the hotel pool. It'll be great!
4 I'm going to make sure my son **will have learned** the alphabet by the time he goes to school. He'll know all the letters.
5 I'm in so much debt I**'ll be paying it off** 'til I'm sixty!
6 I hope we**'ll all be using** renewable energy regularly by the time our natural resources run out.
7 David **will be going** to the tennis club when he finishes his homework.
8 The council **will have spent** its entire budget by the end of summer. They'll have nothing left.

2 **Rob:** What do you think you **(1) 'll be doing** this time next year, Gina?
Gina: Well, by then I **(2) 'll have finished** my final exams, so I think I **(3) 'll be celebrating**! I **(4) 'll be enjoying** my holiday and I **(5) 'll be sunbathing** on a beach somewhere hot. What about you, Rob?
Rob: Well, I've just finished my own studies, so I hope by next June I **(6) 'll have found** a decent job. If I'm lucky, I **(7) 'll be earning** lots of money and I **(8) 'll have bought** myself a car!
Gina: Fingers crossed, then!

Speaking

1 **1** call **2** exact **3** remember **4** thing **5** gone

2 **A** 3/4 **B** 2 **C** 1 **D** 5

3 **1** A **2** A **3** B **4** B
Better answer = B

4 ✓ 3

Reading

2 1 D 2 C 3 B 4 B 5 A 6 C

Grammar

1 1 Sci-fi director Ken Smithies said that as humans we were obsessed with the future.

2 He said that it had taken forty years before the use of mobile phones had become/became widespread.

3 The reporter said that TV reality shows reflected society's fascination with celebrity.

4 Ken reported that most of the film's predictions hadn't come true yet.

5 The scientist asked whether we really wanted to mess with our minds.

6 She told me she was sure that there was still plenty to come from the imaginations of scriptwriters.

2 1 had been doing 2 had interviewed
3 had been taking 4 was going to be
5 would start 6 didn't know 7 was 8 had been

3 1 Jacky said (that) she was planning to take her school exams and then go to college for three years. She said (that) she would really like to study Art History.

2 Jim said (that) he had always wanted to be an actor. He said (that) he would probably go to drama school for a couple of years and then audition for parts on television.

3 Simon said (that) his dream was to be a racing driver in Formula 1, like Lewis Hamilton. He said (that) he had been doing a lot of karting recently and he had won a lot of prizes, so he thought that maybe one day his dream would come true.

Use of English

1 insects, meat, rice

2 1 how 2 with 3 them 4 if/though 5 in
6 of 7 that 8 been

Writing

1 1 aim 2 number 3 said 4 although
5 expected 6 percent 7 appears 8 worth

2 1 It may be worth (8)
2 The aim of this report is (1)
3 It appears from the results (7)
4 A large number (2)
5 Most students said that (3)
6 Fewer students than expected (5)

3 **Sample answer:**

<u>Introduction</u>
The aim of this report is to summarise how students at the college use their phones, following a recent survey.

<u>Talking</u>
Most students use their phones to have conversations with their friends and family every day. A large number of students said that they spend an average of 30 minutes speaking to a friend on the phone in the evening, but calls during the day only last a couple of minutes.

<u>Texting</u>
Surprisingly, fewer students than expected use their phones for texting rather than calling friends. Most students still text a lot, but the majority prefer to speak on the phone. A similar survey last year showed very different results.

<u>Going online</u>
A large number of students have smart phones and go online regularly throughout the day to check emails. They also use this function to buy things and to find out information.

<u>Conclusion</u>
It appears that speaking to people on the phone is still our students' main use of their phones. However, although texting is becoming less popular, going online is increasing and the results of next year's survey may show another big change.

UNIT 10

Reading

1 1 F 2 F

2 1 B 2 C 3 D 4 A 5 B 6 C 7 A 8 A
9 C 10 D

3 1 clapped 2 take 3 sit 4 cheered 5 get
6 went

Grammar

1 1 That's the woman **who** asked me for directions. She's lost.

2 She's the girl **whose** dog ran into our garden.

3 This is the map **which/that** will show you where your hotel is.

4 I suppose I could see you at seven but that's the time **when** I'm normally having dinner.

5 That's the hotel **where** we stayed on our honeymoon.

6 This is the book **which/that** I bought for Sue's birthday.

2 *Many of us have heard of* La Tomatina, *the tomato-throwing festival* **(1) which/that** *is held in Spain each summer – but what really goes on there? Reporter Sue King tells us more …*

La Tomatina is a celebration **(2) where** people take part in the world's largest tomato fight. It takes place on the last Wednesday of August, **(3) when** it starts with the *palo jamón*. The aim of this fun activity is to climb to the top of a pole **(4) which/that** is covered in slippery grease. The leg of ham on top is the prize for the person **(5) who/that** can reach it without sliding back down the pole or falling off. When someone finally grabs the ham, the tomato fight begins. Trucks full of tomatoes enter the town square, **(6) when** they are then thrown at the crowd. These tomatoes come from an area of Spain called Extremadura, **(7) where** they are grown specifically for the festival. The estimated number of tomatoes used in the fight is around 150,000. After exactly one hour, **(8) when** shots are fired from water cannons, the fight ends. The square **(9) where** the fight has taken place is then washed down and the participants, **(10) whose** bodies and faces are now covered in tomato paste, are also provided with water to clean themselves up. See you there next year?!

Speaking

1 **A** 3 **B** 2

2 **A** **1** for **2** because **3** about **4** reason
5 That's **6** instance **7** opinion **8** Don't
B **1** strongly **2** How **3** say **4** like **5** For

3 **1** What about you, Ben?
Don't you think that the books and films sort of …
How do you feel about it, Jack?
2 You know, I'm not really sure.
Sometimes, for me …
I agree.
You know, in my opinion …
Wow! I feel very strongly about this.
I think it's …
I couldn't agree more.
But you're right.
3 That's because I get …
The reason is that a book …
That's why I don't understand …
For instance, the Harry Potter books …
Reading like this helps …
For example, my dad used to …

Listening

1 **1** B **2** C **3** C **4** A **5** B **6** A **7** B **8** C

Vocabulary

1

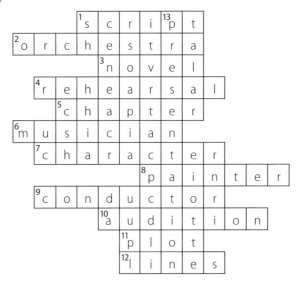

2 **1** script **2** plot **3** orchestra **4** chapters
5 characters **6** novels **7** musician
8 rehearsals, lines

Grammar

1 **1** Tina's going to live in **-** Monte Carlo for a year – she's really looking forward to it.
2 I saw **a** brilliant film last night!
3 Sue had **a** headache yesterday so she didn't go to Mick's party. **The** party was great fun, so it's a pity she missed it.
4 Hotpot is a dish from North West England made from **-** potatoes and lamb.
5 I'm not usually into football but **the** match I saw last night was really exciting.
6 Dan's going to **the** North Pole next summer – how exciting is that?!
7 That's **the** best play I've ever seen.
8 The town's annual music festival will be held in **-** Brown Street this year.
9 This is **the** third time Stacy's been to Scotland. She's from **the** USA and she loves it here.
10 Jim's **an** instructor at a golf course.

2 I'm English, and I get a bit frustrated with the ideas people from other countries have about British food. Lots of visitors to **(1) -** England end up going to fast food restaurants or eat in cheap places where **(2) the** food isn't particularly good and then complain about it. I admit that in the past our meals weren't very exciting – lots of meat and potatoes, or greasy fish and chips. But these days we eat cuisine from all over **(3) the** world. I bet you didn't know that **(4) the** most popular dish in Britain is actually **(5) a** dish called Tikka Masala from **(6) -** India! It contains lots of tasty ingredients like **(7) -** cream and spices and chicken. Italian food is popular, too – you don't have to go far to find **(8) an** excellent restaurant serving up everything from **(9) -** pasta to seafood. But there *are* one or two traditional English meals that even people who aren't British love. How can you beat **(10) a** big plateful of bacon, eggs, sausages and tomatoes, or some delicious roast beef, for example?

Use of English

1   **1** made, do   **2** made, doing   **3** did, doing   **4** making, make   **5** make, making   **6** making, do

2   **1** D   **2** C   **3** A   **4** C   **5** B   **6** D   **7** A   **8** D

Writing

1   A

B is too short; A's title is more interesting; the opening sentence of A is more likely to encourage the reader to continue; in A, 'I'm going to be different!' is lighter

2   **Sample answer:**

When people talk about great writers, they usually mean famous writers from the past whose books are still popular today. However, I'd like to choose a writer whose work is very modern but still influential. Unfortunately, this writer died before his books were published, so he couldn't enjoy their success. I'm talking about the Swedish writer, Steig Larsson.

In my opinion, Larsson's trilogy, which starts with 'The Girl with the Dragon Tattoo', is excellent. He has created some memorable characters and the stories are very clever. In addition to this, he links his plots with Swedish politics, so the books are informative as well as entertaining.

Perhaps the best thing about Larsson's books for me is that each book is different. Yes, the stories have the same characters and the story is developed, but the atmosphere of each book is different. I'm not going to explain any more. You'll need to read them to find out!

UNIT 11

Listening

1   House: 1, 2, 4
Flat: 3, 5

2   **1** F   **2** A   **3** H   **4** B   **5** C

Vocabulary

1   **1** leather   **2** plain   **3** loose

2   **1** fur   **2** tight   **3** leather   **4** striped   **5** material   **6** short-sleeved

3   **1** long, white, silk
2 tight, black, leather
3 floor-length, purple, velvet
4 short-sleeved, checked, cotton
5 fitted, red, leather
6 plain, blue, silk

4   **1** fashionable   **2** genuine   **3** designer   **4** conscious   **5** fake   **6** classic

Grammar

1   **1** E   **2** G   **3** H   **4** C   **5** B   **6** A   **7** D   **8** F

2   Hi, Jim

How are you? I've been really busy. My college organised a fashion show last week to raise money for charity. It was great fun. It **(1) must have taken** ages for the fashion students to make all the clothes. And the music department **(2) must have worked** really hard to create the music they put together for it. They asked me to be one of their models, which was great fun. They **(3) can't have been** bothered about what people looked like because I'm nothing like a model! But it was cool to be asked and everyone who joined in did really well, so the organisers **(4) must have felt** really proud.

The only disadvantage was that I wore my favourite shoes but I don't know where they are now. I **(5) might have left** them in the changing rooms at college, or maybe at a friend's house – I stayed there afterwards. The college **(6) can't have expected** so many people to turn up on the night because there weren't enough chairs in the school hall and loads lots of people had to stand at the back to watch. They sold everything, though and raised a few hundred pounds – well, it **(7) might have been** a thousand, I'm not sure. Anyway, they **(8) can't have made** so much money at a college event before! I've attached a picture of me so you can see how funny I looked.

Write back and tell me all your news!
Mark

Use of English

1   **1** -ance: appearance, assistance
2 -ion: celebration, education
3 -y: dirty, sleepy
4 -ive: attractive, offensive
5 -ness: darkness, fitness
6 -ity: ability, flexibility
7 -ant: accountant, pleasant
8 -ry: bakery, hungry

2   **1** entering   **2** Fortunately   **3** suddenly   **4** unpleasant   **5** suggestions   **6** Luckily   **7** performance   **8** disappointment

Reading

1 unsure whether she likes or dislikes it

2 1 C 2 D 3 B 4 G 5 A 6 F

3 1 short cut 2 originally 3 stunning 4 irritated
5 renewable 6 congestion 7 accessories
8 battle

Grammar

1 1 Wow! That was amazing! I've never seen **such** a good exhibition.

2 We're having our house designed by an award-winning architect – it's **so** expensive, we'll be paying for it 'til we retire!

3 There was a huge storm last night and all the lights went out at home. It was **so** dark we had to light candles.

4 I've broken your favourite mug. I'm **so** sorry! I'll buy you a new one.

5 I saw **such** an interesting programme on TV last night.

6 Denzel's been offered a place at university – he's done **so** well in his exams!

7 There was **such** excitement in the crowd outside the hotel – you just knew that someone really famous was about to turn up.

8 I'd love to study art and design at college, but it's just **so** hard to make a living when you graduate.

2 1 The furniture designs were **very** futuristic. I wouldn't mind having a piece in my home.

2 There weren't **enough** toilets in the venue – maybe you should choose another place next time!

3 I usually like looking at photos but there were **too** many in this exhibition and you had to walk through them all to get to the next room.

4 My kids were **very** pleased with the toy section – I'm bringing them again next time!

5 Great office furniture – I'd order some but it's **too** expensive.

6 I didn't really enjoy this event – it was **very** boring compared with last year's exhibition!

7 The place was certainly big **enough** to hold an exhibition like this, but it was cold and not very inviting.

8 We had to stand up to eat our lunch – there weren't **enough** places to sit in the café. Great show, though.

Speaking

1 1 isn't it 2 do we 3 don't you 4 does it
5 has it 6 will they 7 isn't he 8 won't you

2 1 free time 2 trendy 3 mobile phone
4 last

3 E: Where are you from, Anna?

A: I'm from ~~the~~ Poland. I live in ~~the~~ Warsaw. It is an important city in my country.

E: And you, Katya?

K: I ~~am coming~~ **come** from Russia. My town is very big. I live in **a** big house with my family.

E: What do you like about living in Warsaw, Anna?

A: I ~~am~~ like the people in my town. They are very friendly. The cold and snow aren't good, though! It is always freezing in winter. We must ~~to~~ wear fur coats and thick boots.

E: And what about you, Katya?

K: My town is very pretty. Outside my town there are many trees and nice lakes. There are a lot of things ~~for doing~~ **to do** in the evening too. Cafés, restaurants, ~~walkings~~ **walks** in the parks. I like my town very much.

Writing

1 1 The exhibition is of furniture.

2 It is at the Living Design Museum.

3 It shows how furniture has developed over the last one hundred years.

4 It was interesting for the writer as he/she is studying art and design and is interested in furniture.

2 1 particularly 2 reason 3 favourites 4 display
5 how 6 However 7 thoroughly 8 advice

3 2 – last paragraph should be divided into two

4 **Sample answer:**

Just last week my friend persuaded me to go with her to a fashion exhibition at the Central Museum. I wasn't particularly looking forward to it because it was all about fashion over the last two hundred years. I prefer more modern clothes!

However, I was pleasantly surprised. It was really interesting and focused on the differences between clothes that rich and poor people used to wear in that time period.

I was especially interested in the information in the exhibition guide book. It included a lot of interesting facts about how the clothes were made and where the materials came from. It also told us a lot about the people who designed the clothes for the royal families at that time.

If you're interested in the history of fashion, then I can definitely recommend this exhibition. You can buy tickets online and it is definitely worth doing this as it's very popular. Don't leave it too long because it finishes on the 6th October.

UNIT 12

Reading

1 1 C 2 B 3 D 4 A

2 1 A 2 D 3 B 4 A 5 A 6 C 7 B 8 D
9 C 10 D

3 1 B 2 E 3 F 4 A 5 C 6 D

Grammar

1 1 If no one **had** invented the mobile phone, we
wouldn't have been able to send text messages.
2 I **would** have gone to the science museum with you
if I had known you were going.
3 I wish I **had** come up with an invention that had
changed the world – I'd be famous now!
4 If my parents hadn't bought me a telescope, I
wouldn't **have** become so interested in the stars.
5 If my friend Gary hadn't explained that experiment
to me, I **would** not have got a good mark in my
physics homework.
6 I bet Toni wishes she **had** gone to the talk –
Professor Brian Cox was there!
7 If they hadn't invented the wheel, we **would** not
have developed motor vehicles.
8 I wish I **had** not dropped out of university – I would
have a degree by now.

2 Jenny, 35
I don't know what I **(1) would have done** if they
(2) hadn't invented satellite navigation for cars! I was
never very good at using maps to find my way – my
husband used to make fun of me when I rang him up
because I'd got lost in the middle of nowhere – AGAIN!
So, I decided to get a sat nav for my car, so I wouldn't
have to ring him anymore. I wish I **(3) had got** one
sooner because now I don't need to ask for directions.
I've never told my husband I've got it – I just pretend
I've become an expert map-reader!

Steve, 14
Computer games! I don't play them myself but my
friends spend a lot of time at their computers while
I'm out playing cricket. I've just been accepted into a
sports academy where I'm going to improve my skills.
If no one **(4) had come up with** computer games,
perhaps I **(5) would have had** more competition from
my mates on the sports field!

Tiffany, 16
Thank goodness they invented contact lenses. I've
never minded wearing glasses – in fact, I've got some
really trendy ones, but it can be hard work when
it's raining – you can't see very well and they get all
steamed up. If I **(6) had bought** contacts sooner, I
would have avoided some embarrassing situations.
One day I walked up to a man who I thought was my
boyfriend and gave him a hug! Fortunately, he thought
it was quite funny so it was OK! In fact, he became a
good friend. So if I **(7) had chosen** to get contacts
sooner, I **(8) would have missed** the chance of a good
friendship!

Use of English

1 1 came up 2 keep up with 3 gave away
4 going on about 5 fell through 6 came across

2 1 gave away my 2 I had worked harder
3 keeps going on about 4 keep up with
5 will have found 6 refused to come with me

Listening

1 Jamie Smith, a science teacher. He is talking about
teaching science in schools.

2 1 C 2 C 3 B 4 A 5 A 6 B 7 B

Vocabulary

1 1 F 2 E 3 H 4 B 5 C 6 A 7 D 8 G

2 1 made 2 analyse 3 came 4 conduct 5 take
6 reached 7 done 8 develop

Grammar

1 1 My granddad asked whether I would like to be a
scientist when I left school.
2 She offered to help me carry the/those boxes.
3 The scientist refused to go to the awards ceremony.
4 Our teacher reminded us to wear our goggles.
5 She warned us to be careful because some of the
chemicals were dangerous.
6 Mum apologised for missing/having missed the
concert.

Speaking

1 1 more 2 right 3 wouldn't 4 point
5 disagree 6 partly

2 1 Both 2 on 3 imagine 4 must 5 however
6 like 7 as 8 whereas 9 because 10 can
11 prefer 12 really

Writing

1 1 although 2 In spite 3 However
4 In addition to this 5 As a result 6 Despite

2 1 opinion 2 controversial 3 While 4 in
5 understand 6 However 7 feel 8 In 9 In
10 say

USEFUL LANGUAGE

Invitations and apologies

1 | 1 D 2 A 3 B 4 C

2 | A: Would you like to come?
Do you fancy coming with me?
I'm writing to invite you and Tom …
Would you like to join us?
B: I'd love to.
That would be great.
C: Thank you so much for inviting us.
Thanks for asking me …
D: We would love to come but unfortunately …
I'm afraid I have to work late …

3 | 3

Opinions and agreement

1 | 1 C 2 B 3 E 4 E 5 A 6 D 7 C, A 8 D
9 C, A 10 F

Suggestions, recommendations and advice

1 | 1 to do, talk 2 going, recommend
3 start, do, download 4 do, get
5 to visit, going, go 6 get, get

Requests, offers, permission

1 | 1 B 2 C 3 D 4 A 5 G 6 H 7 F 8 E

2 | Requesting:
Could you …   Would you mind …
I wonder if you could …   Could you please …
Responding to requests:
Certainly.   No problem.
Sure.   Of course.
Offering:
I'll deal with …   Would you like me to …
Responding to offers:
It's OK. Thanks anyway.   That's very kind of you.
Asking for permission:
Can I …   Is it OK if I … ?
Giving/Refusing permission:
That's fine.   Sorry, …

Useful phrases for the Speaking Exam

1 | 1 asking for clarification
2 reminding
3 interrupting
4 adding
5 giving yourself some time to think
6 organising the discussion
7 bringing your partner in
8 speculating

Useful phrases for the Writing Exam

1 | 1 C 2 C 3 B 4 A 5 B 6 C

2 | 1 essay 2 article 3 story 4 essay 5 review
6 review 7 report 8 report 9 review
10 essay

PRACTICE TEST

Paper 1 (Reading and Use of English)

Part 1

1 B 2 A 3 A 4 B 5 C 6 B 7 D 8 A

Part 2

9 However 10 According 11 it 12 more 13 of
14 for 15 is 16 which/that

Part 3

17 endless 18 patience 19 finally 20 broken
21 entertainment 22 delayed 23 wondering
24 exciting

Part 4

25 Vicky said she **wasn't/was not keen on** the pizza.
26 Michael **isn't/is not (very) good at** swimming.
27 Karl **took me by surprise** when he suddenly walked
into the room.
28 A new sports centre **is being built** in the town.
29 One free ride **is included in** the entry ticket to the fair.
30 Mum **reminded me to lock** the door when I left.

Part 5

1 A 2 C 3 B 4 A 5 D 6 D

Part 6

7 F 8 G 9 C 10 A 11 E 12 B

Part 7

13 A 14 D 15 C 16 C 17 D 18 B 19 A
20 B 21 C 22 A

Paper 3 (Listening)

Part 1

1 C 2 A 3 C 4 B 5 A 6 B 7 C 8 B

Part 2

9 sister 10 terrace 11 bracelet 12 statues
13 tourist 14 fashion 15 romantic 16 vegetarian
17 speeches 18 *Sunrise*

Part 3

19 G 20 A 21 B 22 F 23 C

Part 4

24 C 25 A 26 B 27 A 28 C 29 C 30 B

Audio scripts

Unit 1, Listening Activity 1

Track 01

Speaker 1: Like most other people I know, I use a social networking site a lot. I've got loads of friends and I can keep in touch with everyone this way. It's also great to post photos and look at other people's to see what they've been doing! But … you have to be a bit careful. A friend of mine had a really bad experience! She took some time off work to go skiing but she told her boss she was ill! You can guess what happened. She posted photos of herself in Switzerland and someone told her boss! She's looking for another job now!

Speaker 2: I am never separated from my mobile phone! We go everywhere together. I use it at home, at school, in the street – everywhere. That's because I don't like to be out of touch with my friends. But I don't use it on trains now. Last year my boyfriend phoned me while I was on the train and I answered. We often used to chat while I was coming home from school. But this time was terrible. He phoned me because he wanted to finish our relationship! He dumped me and everyone on the train heard the conversation. It all went very quiet. I was *so* embarrassed!

Speaker 3: I know that not many people write letters these days. It takes so long! First, it takes a long time to actually **write** the letter and then it takes ages to arrive! So, usually I email or text. But sometimes I think it's quite nice to send a postcard if I'm on holiday. It's sort of traditional and it's nice to get the picture, isn't it? Well, last year I sent my friend a postcard from Mexico. It was a great picture of a lovely sandy beach. But you won't believe this. It took eighteen months to arrive back in England! I don't know where it went. Probably around the world several times!

Speaker 4: It's so easy to email all your friends. One minute on the computer, press a key and you've done it. But the problem is – it's very easy to make a mistake. We've all done it – written a long email and then clicked the wrong key and it disappears! I made a really *big* mistake last month. I had an argument with my best friend, Eva. It was about something very silly. But I was feeling angry about it. So, I wrote an email to another friend and I told her all about the argument, and I said some bad things about Eva. Well, I sent the email and then I realised … I clicked the wrong key by mistake and I sent the email to everyone in my address book – including Eva! She isn't my best friend anymore!

Unit 2, Speaking Activity 1

Track 02

Examiner: Your pictures show people who have changed their appearance for different reasons. Compare the pictures and say why the people have chosen to change their appearance.

Unit 2, Speaking Activity 2

Track 03

Candidate: Both pictures show people who look different from the way they normally look, but in the first picture the little girl is still changing her appearance whereas in the second picture the people have completely changed already. The little girl is probably getting ready for a party or for a celebration with her friends. I think it might be Hallowe'en or something like that. So, she wants to look different for fun. An older person, it might be her mum, is putting some bright make-up on her face. I think the little girl looks excited! She's probably been looking forward to this for a long time. And little girls always love to dress up! The people in the other picture, however, need to look different because it's their job. They are actors in a play. I think it's a funny play and maybe there's some singing and dancing in it too. They look very happy. Perhaps the audience is clapping. I don't think they needed to change their appearance much – just put on some clothes from a different time and change their hairstyles.

Unit 2, Listening Activity 3

Track 04

Suzy: Winning the lottery has completely transformed my life! I used to ignore all the advertising campaigns for the lottery because I didn't think I would win. But one day, I did my shopping at the supermarket in town and on my way back home I walked past the bookshop near my house. They had a sign outside saying how much you could win, so I decided to give it a go.

However, I forgot all about it until I heard no one had claimed the week's prize. So, I found the ticket in my bag and checked it. I couldn't believe it when I saw that I had the winning numbers. I was so surprised! But after the initial shock, I actually felt worried. I didn't know what I was supposed to do with all that money.

You might think this is strange but whereas most people might go out and buy a big house and a fancy car, I got myself a watch because my old one was broken. It wasn't an expensive one either! It just seemed wrong somehow to go out and spend money on stuff I didn't need.

Then I realised I could help other people and I looked for things to do in my town. I made a donation towards a machine that the hospital needed. I also helped the school I went to when I was young by giving them the money to build a library. That's the thing I feel most proud of. Education's so important.

I helped my family too, of course. My parents needed a new kitchen so I paid for that work to be done and I bought my brother a camera which he was really pleased with because he uses it for his job.

Winning the lottery has definitely transformed my life. I don't have to worry about paying the bills and I know I can help people who need it. I've also had the opportunity to travel abroad for the first time. I went to Spain because I've always wanted to go. Then I paid for my sister and her husband to go to New York and I'm planning to visit Japan one day. Yes, I've been very lucky.

Unit 3, Listening Activities 1 and 2

Track 05

Speaker 1: All types of cookery have become popular recently and that's mainly down to the number of famous chefs on TV. I run a cookery course at the centre and in recent months I've had to start another class too, because it's become so popular! I don't teach everything about cooking, obviously – my course is all about baking – making cakes and biscuits and yummy things like that with loads of calories! You might think that the people who come to my courses are all mums and grannies but you'd be surprised to see the number of teenage boys I have in the class at the moment! They're very good too.

Speaker 2: When you watch those chefs on TV, you would imagine you need to be fairly rich. The items they use to cook that lovely food are very expensive. My class is all about teaching people how to cook really well with very little money. It's amazing how easy it is. When I started the course, I was happy to get five or six students but now the class is full and I have a waiting list. I'm glad it's so popular. I feel as though I'm really helping people at a time when they have to save as much money as they can and that's great.

Speaker 3: Good food is a real pleasure. Most of us enjoy going out for a nice meal. However, these days we also know how dangerous it can be. Putting on weight is a problem. My cookery course tries to help people who have problems with their weight and also their families. I do not run a dieting club! I teach people about food and what it does for our bodies. My students learn how to plan and cook well-balanced meals so that they eat everything they need to be healthy. They lose weight but they also learn eating habits that will help them stay slim.

Speaker 4: My cookery course is aimed at people who want to cook food that is a bit special – not your normal meat and vegetable dishes! I know many students come to the course because they have a real passion for cooking. The TV cooking competitions are to thank for this! People see others just like them cooking amazing meals and think – why not me? So, I show them how. A couple of my ex-students have actually gone on TV competitions since I taught them and one girl – only eighteen – won a major prize. I was very proud!

Unit 4, Speaking Activity 1

Track 06

Examiner: Your pictures show people experiencing different problems while they are travelling. Compare the pictures and say how the people are feeling.

Unit 4, Speaking Activity 2

Track 07

Examiner:
Do you enjoy travelling on the underground?
Do you enjoy travelling by plane?
Do you think it's worse to be delayed at a train station or an airport? Why?

Unit 4, Listening Activities 1 and 2

Track 08

Interviewer: Today we're talking to Monty Saunders, the author of the new book *Who would believe it?* This book is about unusual events that sound more like fiction than fact. It's quite an amazing book, Monty!

Monty: Thank you. I had a lot of fun writing it! I had the idea when I saw a film about how a man managed to survive after a plane crash. I found it fascinating and it started me thinking about how strong our instinct to survive is and I began looking for other interesting survival stories.

Interviewer: I think one of my favourites in the book is the man in the car. Can you tell us something about that?

Monty: Yes – I love this one too. It's quite incredible. It was in the north east of Sweden and two people just passing on snowmobiles thought they had found an abandoned car buried in the snow. They managed to scrape snow and ice off the windscreen and to their amazement they found a man, lying on the back seat of the car. He was alive! Later the man told the police that he'd been there for two months!

Interviewer: But how on earth did it happen?

Monty: Apparently, the man had money problems and he'd broken up with his girlfriend. He was depressed and it's possible he just drove off the main road into a forest area to think about his problems. Then the car got stuck in the snow and he couldn't get out.

Interviewer: I suppose the big question is how did he survive?

Monty: Yes. To live for two months in a car without food or drink is incredible. Also – it was absolutely freezing – the temperatures dropped to –30 degrees during that time. But some doctors believe that the car acted like a sort of igloo – you know, the little houses made of ice where the Eskimos live. Also, he had thick clothing and a good sleeping bag to give him some protection.

Interviewer: But surely people can't live that long without food or water?

Monty: The man has said that he ate handfuls of snow and he had a few basic supplies in the car, like chocolate bars. But apparently it *is* possible to live that long without food. At the end of the period the body has become very thin but you can survive.

Interviewer: I understand that some doctors think there is another explanation for his survival.

Monty: True. Some believe that the human body can lower its temperature when it gets very cold and everything slows down – a bit like animals which go into hibernation for the winter. You don't need to eat or drink. You've read about bears, who go into a cave and sleep all through the winter without food or water? Well, maybe somehow this Swedish man did that! Some experts think differently and say that it's impossible. But nobody really knows.

Interviewer: I guess he was a really lucky guy! Thank you, Monty. And remember listeners, Monty's book is full of more fascinating stories like this one and you can buy it now at all good bookshops! I can thoroughly recommend it.

Unit 5, Listening Activities 1 and 2

Track 09

Extract 1

F: Is that the shirt you bought in the sales? It's really smart.

M: Yeah, that's what *I* thought til I saw the hole in the sleeve – look at that!

F: So, why don't you take it back and get a refund?

M: I can't – they don't give you your money back on sale items. I should have looked at it more carefully before I bought it. Maybe it wasn't such a good deal after all.

F: Oh, no one will notice! It's such a cool brand.

M: Yeah, I guess so. I might ask my mum if she can sew it up for me.

F: Good idea.

Extract 2

F: Wow, look at the jacket in that shop window! I'd love to be able to afford something like that.

M: It's nice, but I don't think designer clothes are worth the money, really.

F: I don't know. If you have the money, why not? The quality's better than the normal chain store stuff.

M: I guess so. Don't you think you're paying a lot for the name, though, rather than anything else?

F: Oh, you can definitely tell the difference between something designer and non-designer, I think.

M: Well, I wouldn't complain if someone bought me a designer gift but if I had money, I'd rather spend it on a good haircut or something I'd wear every day!

Extract 3

M: Good morning, ShoeBox. Can I help you?

F: Yes, I bought a pair of shoes from you the other day and the heel has come off one of them. The only thing is, they were at a discount price in the sale.

M: That's no problem. You'll have to bring them back to the shop, though. Did you keep your receipt?

F: Yes, I think so. Do you need to see it?

M: Yes. We can't exchange the item without it.

F: I'd prefer to get my money back, actually.

M: OK, well, bring the shoes back with the receipt and I'll see what I can do.

F: OK, thank you.

Extract 4

F: Bill Smith, our consumer trends expert is with us on the programme today. Bill, times are difficult. Has this changed the way people shop?

M: Oh, absolutely, yes. The economy is very weak right now and a lot of people have lost their jobs. This means that, instead of doing one big supermarket shop in the same place each week, people are hunting around for bargains – going from shop to shop to find the best deals on products. Shopping online for food has also increased because it means people won't buy those last-minute luxuries at the check-out and can keep an eye on how much they're spending more easily.

Extract 5

F: I'm trying to save up to buy a car, so I won't be coming out as much at the weekends.

M: Really? But you love going out! And it'll take you ages to save that much money!

F: Yeah, I'm going to cut down on how much I spend on clothes, too. I love fashion but I've decided to buy one or two more expensive things that will last, rather than lots of cheap things that I'll throw away after I've worn them a couple of times.

M: Makes sense. But won't you get fed up wearing the same things?

F: Well, I won't be going out as much so it won't matter!

Unit 5, Speaking Activity 3

Track 10

Student A: So, let's think about leaflets first. Is that a good way of advertising? What do you think?

Student B: Mmm. They're quite quick and easy to do – and they won't cost too much. But don't you think that a lot of people will just throw them away?

Student A: I know what you mean. If you get a leaflet, you often don't even look at it! Especially if it comes through the door.

Student B: How about a radio commercial? Loads of people listen to the radio.

Student A: You're right. Dad always has it on in his car. But it might be a bit expensive.

Student B: It depends. We could always record it ourselves – we wouldn't have to pay actors!

Student A: And that would be great fun! OK – that's a possibility. Then, of course, there are posters. I'm sure the school could produce those.

Student B: And we could go round sticking them up in shop windows. People usually look at posters – particularly if they're bright and clever. The art students could design some good ones.

Student A: Cool! And the newsletter advert would be good. It won't cost anything.

Student B: Yeah. But it only goes to school students and families, doesn't it? We need to get to a wider audience.

Student A: So, maybe the advert in the local paper is a good idea. People often browse through the 'What's on?' section when it gets near the weekend.

Student B: Good idea. How about the T-shirts? I really like the idea – but it would cost a lot.

Student A: But then if all the organisers wear a T-shirt advertising the sale for a few weeks before, people will notice, won't they?

Student B: I'm not too sure about that. It will only really be their friends and family and they'll know anyway! I think you just want a free T-shirt!

Student A: *[laughs]* Why not?!

Examiner: Now you have a minute to decide which form of advertising should not be used.

Student A: OK, so which do you think we shouldn't use?

Student B: For me, it's the T-shirts. They're expensive.

Student A: Oh, I really like the idea. You can keep T-shirts afterwards to remember the event. Everyone loves T-shirts! We could even make more and sell them! But I'm really not sure about the leaflets.

Student B: Yeah – I think you're right. Also – someone's got to go round putting them in people's doors too! I don't fancy that – particularly if it's raining!

Student A: OK. I agree. Let's forget about the leaflets.

Unit 6, Speaking Activities 1 and 2

Track 11

Student A: Let's start with the firefighter, shall we? He's got a really dangerous job because he might easily get hurt while he's working.

Student B: That's true. It's their job to put out fires and to rescue people, so every day they risk their lives.

Student A: But firefighters are well trained, aren't they? They know when to go into a burning building and when not to.

Student B: Yeah. They must really love their job. They actually save people's lives.

Student A: The chef's a bit different, isn't he? The danger in his job isn't that bad. Do you agree?

Student B: Yes – but you know, things go wrong in kitchens – they get fires there too and maybe they eat bad food.

Student A: I think the biggest danger for a chef is stress. Chefs always have very red faces and they rush round all the time in a hot place. A lot of them get heart problems.

Student B: Absolutely.

Student A: What about police officers? I wouldn't like to be a police officer today. A lot of criminals have guns and knives.

Student B: Yes, it's dangerous. A lot of police officers get hurt and sometimes even killed. But also, people don't always like the police! So, although it's good to catch the bad guys, they're also unpopular.

Student A: You're right. People blame the police if they don't catch the criminals but they also complain about them if they arrest the wrong people. They can't win.

Student B: No. The photographer has a great job, I think. It can be dangerous when you're trying to get good pictures of wild animals. You have to go to really wild and unsafe places to get the best pictures. Sometimes they have to climb up the sides of mountains or even go underwater.

Student A: Yes – and if you're filming a lion or something like that, it might attack you! Or underwater, think of the sharks and whales!

Examiner: Now you have a minute to decide which job is the most rewarding.

Student A: Obviously, it's good to save people like the fire fighters do and arrest the bad guys like the police officers, don't you think?

Student B: Yeah. I actually think that chefs have a rewarding job too. They're creative and they know that people like their work.

Student A: Too much, sometimes!

Student B: I think all dangerous jobs are rewarding in some way because you must feel like you've achieved something! For me, it's got to be the photographer.

Student A: Yeah. What a job! To go to all those brilliant places – even under the sea. I don't think they bother about the danger. And if they know their job well – it isn't too dangerous.

Student B: OK. Let's go for the wildlife photographer.

Unit 6, Listening Activities 1 and 2

Track 12

Zena: I've loved watching movies for as long as I can remember, and I used to sit on my mum's knee watching the romantic films she liked. I loved them too. My dad liked action films and when I was in my teens I got into those too; in fact, I loved them so much I wanted to be one of the people who performed the stunts. And that's where it all began.

The profession is quite different now to how it used to be. The earliest stunt people weren't given any training and just had to learn through trial and error how to perform stunts. Modern action movies didn't exist at that time, so most work was in comedies, you know, like falling off a wall or something silly like that!

I didn't really think about working in the film industry until I was taking karate classes. I was doing pretty well and my teacher suggested I auditioned for a part in a film where the producer was looking for people with skills in martial arts to perform some stunts. I eventually persuaded my mum to let me have a go and I got the part! The rest is history.

You don't really need acting skills to do the job – which you might expect – but you do need to be very fit. Climbing or being able to ski can be really useful skills to have too – anything that will help you stand out from the crowd, really.

Working as a stunt person can be very competitive. You don't need a 'stunt degree' or anything, but you can get into the industry by being a film extra – a kind of actor who plays very small parts in a film, like walking down a street appearing to be shopping or something. This gets you familiar with film sets and you might get to meet the stunt coordinators who may give you work.

Being a stunt person isn't a glamorous job, like some people think, but it's really exciting and you get to work with some great people. The best job I've done was working as a double for a famous film star who didn't want to perform her own stunts. I was fortunate to be the same height as her with a similar figure. My hair wasn't the same though, so I had to wear a wig to look a bit more like her!

It's taken a long time for women to enter the industry, so I was really excited when I won an award for my work. It was only a little statue – no cash or anything – but it got me recognised and now I'm busier than ever!

Unit 7, Speaking Activity 2

Track 13

I like these pictures! It's good to see people who are enjoying life. Both the young guy with the iPod and the family look very happy. The guy has a contented smile on his face and the family are laughing. But the reasons they are happy are probably quite different. I mean, the young guy is listening to music, he's alone but his eyes are closed so you can imagine that he's lost in his world of music. He might be in a park or relaxing in his back garden, but he's definitely away from all the stresses of life! The family, on the other hand, are in a busier place. They are probably on holiday and they seem to be enjoying a meal outside together. For them and the boy, the weather looks good. I'm sure the family are happy because they're together and relaxing and maybe someone has told a joke! It must be very enjoyable and exciting to eat a meal in a lovely place like that!

Unit 7, Listening Activities 1 and 2

Track 14

Speaker 1: It seems to me that it isn't really worth going to see the doctor these days! There are so many programmes on television about different illnesses and how to avoid getting them, or what to do if you've got them! Why bother going to see a specialist? In my opinion, these programmes are really useful and I always watch and note down different things. I mean, who knows when you might catch something? Also, I like them because you get lots of information about unusual illnesses. There are interviews with people all over the world with health problems that you don't know anything about. It's important to be informed, don't you think?

Speaker 2: I have to admit that I hate going to the doctor. In my experience, doctors don't really help you very much unless you've got something really bad and then they just send you on to see someone else! I prefer to get help from someone who knows a lot about health problems – because she's seen many of them during her life. That's my grandmother! She can always tell me what to do if I've got a cough or a headache! And her treatment is simple and usually works. She has a lot of old stories about what to do with different illnesses, stories that *her* mother told *her*! Like drinking special tea made of flowers when you've got a cold. Or putting a special herb on a cut to make it heal faster. She's ninety-six now, so I think she knows what she's talking about!

Speaker 3: When I had a pain in my hand, a friend of mine advised me to go online and check out a website. I was going to the doctor but he said you can get good advice from websites. It was very interesting. The website advice was good – but the best thing was all the comments people had posted about their problems. Some of them had exactly the same problem as me! I followed the advice they gave and in two days my hand was better. I know you have to be careful and if things don't get better, it's important to go to the doctor. But this advice certainly helped. My friend also said that his doctor usually looks online anyway when he goes with a problem – probably at the same websites!

Speaker 4: My mother always kept a book about illnesses and treatments when I was young. Every time I hurt myself or had a high temperature, she would look in the book and follow the instructions! She gave it to me when I left home as a present! I have to say that it is very useful. It tells you when you need to see a doctor and when you can treat yourself. It's easy to understand too – without lots of difficult medical words! I know that scientists are developing more and more ways to treat illnesses but the basic problems and cures don't really change, do they?

Unit 8, Listening Activities 1 and 2

Track 15

Interviewer: Michelle, you're seventeen and have a guide dog. Tell us about your dog, Rufus.

Michelle: Yes, because I can't see very well I have a guide dog who helps me get around. You could say he's my eyes! I'd never had a dog before so when I first got him, I wasn't sure how to behave around him but he's so lovely and friendly, it was easy. I wondered if he might get a bit fed up doing nothing if I was just chilling out at home but he's really patient. I knew he'd be intelligent, though, or he wouldn't have become a guide dog. If I'm out walking and I want to go home, I just say 'Home, Rufus!' and he takes me straight there!

Interviewer: Did you have to do any training with him?

Michelle: Yes, I had to learn quite a few different things, like feeding him and brushing him, which wasn't too hard, but there were a lot of commands to learn – you know, like what to say to get him to do what I wanted. I kept forgetting them at first and I think he got a bit confused! I also learned how important it is to let him off the lead to go and run around for a bit and have fun – he's not allowed to do that while he's working. I was worried he might run off and never come back – but of course, he always did.

Interviewer: What difference has having a guide dog made to your life?

Michelle: Oh, it's completely changed my life! I'm much more independent now and don't have to rely on my parents to take me places. That means they get more free time too, so it's good for everyone. I guess the greatest change has been just not being so frightened when I'm out. I used to worry about stepping onto the road but I know Rufus won't let me do that. Also, lots of people stop and talk to me when I'm with Rufus, so it's nice to have that social contact.

Interviewer: How did the trainers decide that Rufus was the dog for you?

Michelle: Well, I had a visit from the guide dog organisation and they spent some time with me, talking to me about my life and finding out a bit about my personality, things like that. I like going out and doing things so they found a dog that would enjoy that. You're also assessed to see how fast you walk. I don't walk too quickly, so they found me a dog that would be happy at my speed. I'm quite tall as well, so it wouldn't have been much good if they'd given me a small dog!

Interviewer: And Rufus goes to college with you, doesn't he?

Michelle: Yeah, and he loves it! He comes to most of my classes, though when I do science, he stays with a carer because he might get scared by noises or heat in the lab. My friends love him but I do have to keep reminding them not to play with him or feed him because he might get distracted when he's supposed to be working. He can't respond when he's concentrating on looking after me but I know he'd love the attention if he could!

Interviewer: What do you like most about Rufus?

Michelle: Oh, he's a great dog! I love spending time with him. My favourite thing about being with him is when I get home from college and we spend time messing about in the garden – he's got a great sense of humour and when he's off his lead he does all kinds of silly things which make me laugh. He always knows how I'm feeling too and he comes and comforts me when I need him to. My family love him and I feel so lucky to have him.

Unit 8, Speaking Activity 1

Track 16

Examiner: Here are some things people can do to help the environment. Talk to each other about how these things can help the environment.

[Pause]

Now you have a minute to decide which is the most important.

Unit 8, Speaking Activity 2

Track 17

A: So, we have to say how these things can help the environment. Is that right?

B: OK, well, obviously recycling your rubbish is really important. It helps because then we don't put so much stuff into landfill sites.

A: What do you mean, 'landfill'?

B: That's what they call those great big rubbish dumps in the countryside. You know, the rubbish stays there for ages.

A: OK. Yeah – we reuse things and don't have to use energy and new materials to make things from scratch.

B: You mean – like clothes and things?

A: Exactly. What about the food for birds? Do you think that's very helpful?

B: Well, yes. Because with climate change a lot of bird species are dying out.

A: Sorry, I don't understand.

B: Sometimes the winters are harder and they can't find food, or the summers are hotter and they don't get enough water.

A: So, are you saying that it's more important to feed birds than recycle rubbish?

B: No, I'm just pointing out that a lot of our wildlife is having a bad time and it's good to help, don't you agree?

A: Could you say that again?

B: It's good to help …

A: Sorry, I meant the bit about the wildlife.

Unit 9, Listening Activities 1 and 2

Track 18

As you know, we've all been asked to come up with a design for a house of the future in our science and technology class, so I want to show you mine and tell you all about it. I've come up with a few ideas which I think could be put into practice.

Builders have traditionally used natural materials, such as wood and stone, but in the future, I think we'll be using new materials which will be stronger, more weather resistant and much more energy efficient, which means that as well as protecting against things like rainwater damage, heating bills will be much cheaper.

Every home will also be fitted with all kinds of machines and equipment like solar panels and wind turbines, which will help to create our homes' own energy. I also believe we'll have a recycling machine which will sort out all our glass and plastic and will even be able to clean water so that we can use it again.

Our cupboards will still be full of delicious food, but while we're already starting to take reuseable shopping bags with us when we go shopping, in the future supermarkets will have learned how to reduce the amount of packaging they use, which will be better for the environment and make food cheaper too.

That's all I'm going to say on the topic of the environment, but I've also come up with some inventions which will make our lives easier. For example, instead of having to wash sheets and duvet covers, we'll be using a special kind of sleeping bag. This can be washed as a single item because the pieces are all sewn together.

And you know how we've already got self-cleaning dishwashers? Well, we'll also have washing machines that do the same things. I'm also working on an idea for a self-cleaning bathroom. You'll shut the door, press a button and everything will be done for you! No more weekend chores!

And what if you lose your keys and feel worried that someone will find them and let themselves in? Well, we'll all have a voice recognition box outside our front door, which will automatically let us into the house when we speak to it. No need for burglar alarms either, as automatic shutters will come down over windows if they realise someone is trying to break in.

As the world's population grows and more people live alone, we'll need more housing but will have less space for it, so we'll need a lot of space-saving devices. I've designed a cool desk that turns into a dining table and a cooker that has a microwave oven built into it, which is my best invention so far and I'm really pleased with myself. And of course, there will be sofas that turn into beds.

What about cooking? Well, we'll still do it, of course – everyone loves eating – but instead of standing in a hot kitchen for hours, we'll have a pot where we'll put all the ingredients, programme in the dish we want to eat and it will do everything for us. No more chopping vegetables or stirring sauces.

The fridge will be able to connect to the internet, so it will know when we're getting low on our favourite foods and order them for us. The grass will be cut by an automatic lawnmower, which will mean Dad can watch the football instead, which he'll do online on his large-screen computer rather than on a TV.

And while he's doing that, Mum will be able switch off more easily by putting on a helmet that will be able to read her mind and remove any negative thoughts running around in there, so she can get some peace! In the meantime, I'll put on my exercise suit and watch TV while it gets my body in shape! I hope you've enjoyed my talk on homes of the future. Any questions?

Unit 10, Speaking Activity 2

Track 19

A

Anna: OK, let me think. You know, I'm not really sure. Sometimes, for me, it's better to read the book first. That's because I get my own pictures in my head about the characters. What about you, Ben?

Ben: Yes, I like to read the book. The reason is that a book is not only about what happens, the story or plot – it's the way it's written, how the writer makes us imagine the pictures. A film is different.

Anna: I agree. That's why I don't understand people who say 'It wasn't as good as the book.' I'm not sure we should compare them because they're different.

Ben: For instance, the Harry Potter books and films. Children read and loved the books but they got pleasure from the films for different reasons.

Anna: You know, in my opinion, that's a special example. Don't you think that the books and films sort of led into each other?

Ben: That's a good point.

B

Eva: Wow! I feel very strongly about this. I think it's very important for parents to read to their children. It helps their imaginations to grow. When I was young, my mum read to me every night and I looked forward to it a lot. How do you feel about it, Jack?

Jack: I couldn't agree more. It also helps the relationship between parent and child. I say that because sometimes it's the only time in the day that they have the chance to have time together. But you're right. Reading like this helps children in so many ways. For example, my dad used to read me adventure stories and I loved them so much I couldn't wait to learn to read myself.

Eva: And you haven't stopped since! He's always got his head in a book!

Unit 10, Listening Activity 1

Track 20

Extract 1

M: Hi there! Your new play must be starting soon. I'm definitely going to book a ticket to see you.

F: Actually – it started last night.

M: Really? I'm so sorry – I wanted to wish you good luck. How did it go?

F: It was amazing! Every ticket was sold – we were completely full! The audience loved it.

M: Well done! It's only on for a week, isn't it? I'll try to come on Thursday.

F: Yes, we finish on Saturday night. You'd better book today because it's really popular and I know that Friday is full too.

M: I'll do that. Good luck for the rest of the week.

Extract 2

M: What did you think about the programme on the graffiti art exhibition last night?

F: I enjoyed it a lot. I've always liked that art style and I thought it was a great idea to have the show in the street and not in a gallery.

M: I know. I especially liked the pictures that an artist had done on the outside walls of the old hotel.

F: I agree – it was a bit different. I wonder where you can buy art like that. I'd like to get some for my room.

Extract 3

It's another public holiday and another busy day on the roads for drivers. Police wanted people to try to set off at different times today to avoid the big traffic jams we usually get on public holidays. Unfortunately, this hasn't happened and so we have heavy traffic on all the major routes, particularly in the south west. An accident near the Matcham's car festival in Ferndown has closed the A31 and motorists are asked to find a different route. Traffic is also heavy in the area near Bournemouth airport, so if you are planning to catch a flight, please allow more time for your journey.

Extract 4

M: I did enjoy the meal last night. Thank you very much for inviting me.

F: Thanks for coming! It is a great restaurant, isn't it? I think it's the best seafood restaurant in town.

M: You're right. My fish was cooked perfectly. But I had a bad stomach during the night.

F: I hope the fish didn't make you ill!

M: Oh no. I'm allergic to salmon, but I was careful to avoid that. I was just greedy and I had a big dessert as well.

F: I once had to go to hospital after eating bad fish in a restaurant. It must always be very fresh.

M: That is so true!

Extract 5

M: Mary? It's Charlie. I know you said you were busy tonight but we really need someone for the quiz team. David has to take his daughter to a music competition, so there are only three of us and he said I should ask you. Is there any chance you could come? Last year we won first prize when you were on the team! It would be great to do that again. It starts at 7.30 and should be over by nine. Do let me know if you can make it! I'm on 07789 785643. Thanks.

Extract 6

F: I hear you went to the Karen Webb sculpture exhibition in Margate last week?

M: Yeah – I went with my brother just before it finished.

F: I wanted to go but I've been a bit busy recently and it's a long way, isn't it? I wish I'd gone now.

M: You'd have loved it. But you're right – it took us hours to get there and back. They had the exhibition there because Webb lived for most of her life in the town.

F: I know. I've read some books about her work. I really like her style and the materials she uses.

M: Me too.

Extract 7

M: My French friend wants me to recommend an English book for her to read in English. What do you think about a detective novel?

F: Yes, if she's got a good level, that would be perfect.

M: I think she's been studying English for about a year.

F: In that case, I think something like a special English book for learners might be better. You can get good, interesting stories in easy English.

M: Yeah – good idea. I was thinking about a children's book, but she might find that a bit boring. I could suggest the detective novel for later on.

Extract 8

M: I started buying books and DVDs online quite a while ago. At first I wasn't sure if delivery would go smoothly. You know, whether things might get delayed in the post or even disappear. And people had warned me about getting the wrong books. In fact I've found it a very good system. Everything I've ordered has turned up – apart from one book that was a bit damaged in the post and they just sent me another one free when I complained! I like buying things this way because it's quicker and easier. I can order a book today and it arrives in a couple of days' time! And it doesn't cost any more than in a shop – sometimes less.

Unit 11, Listening Activities 1 and 2

Track 21

Speaker 1: I suppose we all thought it was going to be hard, moving from a big house to a much smaller one. I used to have an enormous room at the old place and I really didn't want to have to throw away a lot of my things because they didn't fit into the new one. At first sight, it looked as if I was right, but strangely enough the new room has been designed really well and there's actually loads of space for all my clothes and computer, TV and so on. I'd prefer to look out over the garden, instead of the road but it's nowhere near as bad as I'd thought. And it's got an amazing red carpet too!

Speaker 2: We moved in a month ago but it still doesn't feel like home yet! It's a very modern building with three floors, my room is on the top floor and everything is new and clean and up-to-date. We've got computer monitors in every room and the latest equipment in the kitchen. It's very high tech, which is great! I do miss the open fire in the living room we used to sit round, but I suppose I'll get used to it. At first I wasn't sure about the stone floor in the kitchen – it looks good, but I thought it might be a bit cold on the feet. Actually, it's the opposite!

Speaker 3: Our new flat in the city is brilliant! It's on the first floor and is right by a park. I spend ages just looking at the birds across there! The flat has lots of windows so it's very light and airy. Also, there are a lot of open spaces. Like – the kitchen area leads into the living area – with no walls and not many cupboards. What bothers me is not that it can get very untidy – although that is a problem sometimes! It's more that – apart from my bedroom there are no places you can just enjoy a quiet moment! I go across to the park when I want to be on my own.

Speaker 4: I was hoping for a big room when we moved to quite a large house in the country last year and I was very happy when I saw it! It's very spacious, with big old windows and I can see right across the fields to the village. There aren't many places to put things, though and half my clothes are in my sister's room because she's got bigger cupboards than me. It means that my room gets a bit messy with clothes over the chairs. Still, I'm happy with it. The walls are also nice and thick and although I can sometimes hear my sister's TV, it's usually peaceful in there.

Speaker 5: I love the design of our new flat. It's small but it's got everything you need. It's in the middle of town so it can be a bit noisy during the day and there aren't any trees or grass to look at! Still, I don't spend much time looking out of windows! My mum loves the wooden floors because they're easy to keep clean but I'd like to persuade her to get a carpet because somehow they make a room feel warmer, don't you agree? I know we've got good radiators but it's more about atmosphere, really.

Unit 11, Speaking Activity 2

Track 22

1

Examiner: How do you like to spend your free time?

Student: I usually go out with friends or read a book. I enjoy reading. Sometimes at the weekends, I work out at the gym.

2

Examiner: Would you say that you are a trendy person?

Student: I think so. I like to buy the latest designer clothes. When I've got enough money! And I keep up-to-date by reading magazines.

3

Examiner: How important is your mobile phone?

Student: Oh – very. I couldn't live without it! I call or text my friends all the time and I keep all my mates' addresses and numbers on it too.

4

Examiner: What was the last film you went to see?

Student: I haven't seen anything for a while. But I think it was something with Will Smith in. It had really good special effects but I can't remember the name.

Unit 12, Listening Activities 1 and 2

Track 23

Interviewer: Today, on *School Matters*, I'm talking to science teacher, Jamie Smith. Jamie, why did you become a science teacher?

Jamie: I became a science teacher because I loved science lessons at school. This wasn't because I found science itself so interesting but because of my teacher. He'd start off every new topic by doing a magic trick which used scientific principles to work. He would never tell us how he did the trick, but if you paid enough attention to the experiments and things we talked about in class, you'd be able to figure it out. He made me want to be a teacher and because the things he did stuck in my head, I decided to go into science myself.

Interviewer: What do you like best about teaching science?

Jamie: There are some useful teaching materials available and some great books that the students love. It makes teaching easier. It's that element of discovery, though, isn't it? Watching the kids work it out for themselves. I love the expression on their faces when they suddenly get an idea – you can see them thinking, 'Oh! *That's* how it works!'

Interviewer: Which science subject do you most enjoy teaching?

Jamie: My favourite science as a kid was chemistry – I had a science kit at home and used to do experiments in the garage with my dad. That gave me a real thrill and it's something that I still love passing on to kids. Physics is inspiring, the way it helps to explain the universe but it's based on theory and there's a lot of maths in it, which can be tricky for some, and that makes it less enjoyable to teach. Everyone loves biology because they're familiar with what's being talking about – that takes a bit of the excitement away for me, though.

Interviewer: What do you find difficult about teaching science?

Jamie: Well, you always get those kids who just want to mess around in class – they break expensive equipment and throw chemicals around. That can be a pain. Also, the school I work in has very limited resources, so we can't buy all the best equipment, which is a shame. Most frustrating of all, though, is when I see a kid trying their best to get their head around a problem and just not getting there. That's when I get frustrated. Not at them, but for them.

Interviewer: And you're going to submit an entry to the science fair, is that right?

Jamie: Yes! We've created an eco-car that runs on vegetable juice! I know that sounds strange but it really does work. I think we have as good a chance as anybody else to win, but you just never know what other schools are going to come up with. I'm trying to get through to the students working on the project that they should focus on the fun they're having rather than on the possible prize at the end of it, but all they can think about is winning. I don't want them to be too disappointed if we don't.

Interviewer: Why do you think science is so important in schools?

Jamie: Well, it explains things, doesn't it? I mean, you can actually prove stuff by demonstrating it and working things out and that's pretty useful. Above all, there's always something different on the horizon, something new to find out. I also think it helps students to develop thinking skills and creativity and those are things you can use in other subjects.

Interviewer: What scientific discovery would you like to have made?

Jamie: Oh, I wish I'd discovered some kind of medicine that would cure everything. How exciting would that be? It's not because I'd have become famous or anything like that, it's just the idea of doing something that has changed people's lives for the better. I don't work in medical science so it's unlikely I'll ever do anything like that now, but I'm definitely encouraging some of my students to go into medicine and do it for me!

Unit 12, Speaking Activity 1

Track 24

Extract A

A: The light bulb was important because it meant that people could stay up later!

B: I couldn't agree more. It also meant that there weren't so many fires from candles and lamps.

A: You're absolutely right.

Extract B

A: I don't think that spectacles were particularly important, do you? It didn't change the way people lived.

B: I wouldn't say that. It helped a lot of people continue their jobs and enjoy their lives better.

A: OK. I agree up to a point. But I don't think that invention was as important as, say, the light bulb.

Extract C

A: For me, the most important invention was the telephone. It let people contact each other from long distances.

B: I completely disagree with you! In my opinion, it was the computer. Look how it's changed everybody's lives today.

A: I partly agree with you – but you see, without the telephone I don't think we would have the computer, would we?

B: OK. I see what you mean!

Unit 12, Speaking Activity 2

Track 25

A: OK. Both pictures show people who have got scientific jobs but the sort of jobs are very different. In the picture on the left, an astronaut is out in space. I imagine he's doing a space walk. They sometimes do this to repair the space ship. He must have a lot of knowledge about science but he's doing a practical job. The man on the right, however, is in a classroom or lecture room and he's teaching some students about science. He's showing them an experiment or something like that. I don't think his job is as exciting as the astronaut's because he's always in a classroom, whereas the astronaut goes to fantastic places. He can see things that not many people have seen. It's dangerous because a lot of things can go wrong, but I think it's more interesting than being a teacher!

B: I'd prefer to work in a classroom because I'd be really scared to be up in space!

Practice test Paper 3, Listening Part 1

Track 26

Extract 1

The flight itself was actually OK, in spite of all my nerves! There was quite a lot going on, you know, meals, drinks, shopping trolley and as well as that, they had some very recent films to watch, so I didn't really notice the time pass. I thought I was going to be terrified on take-off, but as it turned out I was more excited than scared. It's such a cool experience! I hope I get to fly again sometime soon. It was a shame that we had to wait around at the airport because of the snow. Without that, it would have been a perfect journey.

Extract 2

Hi, Jen. I know we agreed to meet up for lunch around twelve thirty, but something's come up at work and I'm not going to be able to get away for at least another hour. I've got a feeling that you need to be back at college for two o'clock, so it would make our lunch quite short! Perhaps we ought to leave it for a couple of days. What do you think? Text me when you get this message because I'll be in a meeting and I'll ring you back later. Speak soon!

Extract 3

A: You've been getting excellent reviews for your performance in *Hamlet*. Congratulations! But people don't usually think of you as a Shakespearean actress, do they?

B: I know what you mean. I suppose I'm better known for my roles in soap operas on television! This was my first Shakespeare role for twenty years. I'm not too sure why – I suppose it's because Shakespeare is very difficult to do well. I turned down a couple of parts a few years ago but then I was asked by Michael Barnes, a director who I very much admire, to take on this part. There was no way I could turn down such an opportunity.

A: Well, we're all very glad you accepted the offer!

Extract 4

It's perfectly normal to get a bit scared before a race. In fact, it's much better for your performance to have a few butterflies, it gets the adrenaline going and your body goes faster. As a competitor, you learn to cope with that. So, that wasn't a problem for me last week. I'd done a lot of training and I was on good form, in line for the gold medal. Standing on the blocks, ready to dive in, was an exciting moment. Then the whistle went and I was in the air – splash – into the water. It was a very good start, one of my best. But no one else was with me! It hadn't been the starter's whistle but someone in the crowd. Did I feel bad! Of course, my confidence went then and I didn't win.

Extract 5

A: Did you get those jeans in the sales yesterday?

B: Yeah. I went in with Bill just before lunch yesterday, but it was a nightmare. The mall was jammed with people looking for bargains and getting frustrated because they couldn't find any. There are some good reductions but you have to look for them. I got the jeans I wanted at a great price. But when you go, avoid the main car parks because they'll be full. In fact, I'd take the bus. We had a real problem getting anywhere near the mall. And try not to get there after ten thirty. You won't be able to move!

A: Cheers. I'm having second thoughts about going at all. I may give them a miss this time.

Extract 6

A: I wasn't that impressed by the first episode of the new Agatha Christie series on TV last night. I'm not too sure why. It's got a fantastic cast. Did you see it?

B: Yeah, but I feel the same. I think it's the way they've set it in the present day. For me, the story and the characters are all part of that time – the thirties or forties – when Christie originally wrote them. Christie's ladies should be wearing fur coats and have cigarette holders – not romping around town in jeans and boots.

A: That's it. Mind you, I'm going to watch next week's episode – I just love the guy who plays the detective. Maybe I'll get used to the setting!

Extract 7

In spite of the weather warnings issued for the region yesterday morning, many people ignored advice to stay at home and, as a result, found themselves stranded in their cars because of dangerously icy conditions and roads blocked by minor accidents and snow. The strong winds have also brought down some power lines and at the moment, more than a thousand houses in the area are without electricity. Engineers are doing their best to restore services but it is thought that some people will have to do without power for at least another forty-eight hours. More snow and winds are forecast for tomorrow and Friday, with milder weather coming in for the weekend.

Extract 8

A: So, how's your new laptop?

B: I was really pleased with it when I first got it. It's so small and light, I can take it anywhere – unlike my last one! Sometimes, however, it takes ages to connect. Yours is the same model as mine, does yours do that, too?

A: Not now, but it was doing something similar last year. My brother, Matt, had a look at it and it's been running better since then. Shall I ask him to give you a ring? It's better than taking it back to the shop. They just send it away and you won't have it for months.

B: Great. Thanks.

Practice test Paper 3, Listening Part 2

Track 27

I'm going to tell you about my cousin's wedding in Paris. The whole family had been invited. I was excited because I'd never travelled abroad before and I was looking forward to taking the trip with my parents. My sister was disappointed not to go but she was preparing for her exams, so she had to stay at home and look after the dog!

We arrived in Paris the night before the big day. The hotel was good, though the website we'd booked it on said there was a terrace but it was actually just a disappointing strip of pavement on the busy road. The rooms were nice, though we didn't have a good view from the window – we looked out over the dustbins at the back of the hotel!

The next day, we got up early to get ready for the day. I thought I'd packed everything I wanted to wear for the wedding – I'd coordinated everything from my hairband to my sandals, so you can imagine how irritated I was to find that I'd left my bracelet behind. It didn't really matter, but my cousin had bought it for me as a present and I wanted to wear it for the occasion.

We set off to the Town Hall for the wedding. I couldn't wait to see the bride and I wondered whether French weddings were similar to the ones back home. The room was full of beautiful flowers – it was the statues that drew my attention, though. They were unlike anything I'd seen before. There were some good paintings too, though not so spectacular – it was such a lovely room to get married in.

My cousin looked beautiful and the service brought a tear to my eye. Afterwards, we filed outside where the photographer took loads of pictures of the happy couple. There were loads of people around and I spotted a tourist taking photos too – it really added to the atmosphere. There was even a journalist there who knew my cousin – he was going to write an article about the wedding!

My cousin had organised a surprise for the guests before the reception. We were taken on a sightseeing tour of the city! It was good to see the monuments, though I'd seen lots of pictures of them already. What was *really* thrilling was looking at what everyone was wearing – Paris is known for its fashion and I'm really into it. I'd love to go back and do some shopping there!

After the tour, we went to the restaurant where the reception was taking place. It had a fabulous view overlooking the river – it was so romantic. There was a band that played cool, jazz music and the tables were covered in decorations. My cousin and her new husband had done a really good job of deciding where to hold their wedding celebration.

Then we sat down for the wedding meal – I'd never eaten food quite like it. France is renowned for its cuisine and I wasn't disappointed. I'm a vegetarian and they'd made a dish especially for me. Everyone else had seafood, which I'd love to have tried but I'm allergic to it, so I couldn't. But the dessert was amazing!

At English weddings, there are speeches. This is where people talk about the couple. It's my favourite part of a wedding so I was a bit taken aback that it didn't happen at this one. I don't know why. They did do a first dance, though, where the couple danced to one of their favourite songs and everyone stood by, clapping and cheering.

For the rest of the evening, we danced and I had the time of my life. They played all my favourite music, including my top tune of all time, *Sunrise*. There was a DJ who you could give requests to – my dad asked for all the old stuff like *Raindrops*, and he danced around like a teenager – embarrassing! Anyway, I've brought some pictures along if anyone wants to see them?

Practice test Paper 3, Listening Part 3

Track 28

Speaker 1: I'm a big fan. I've read nearly all her books once and several of them twice or more! In fact, I started reading them when I was still at high school. I remember having one open on my lap while I was supposed to be working in class! I'm not too sure exactly why I picked up the first book – it could be because I saw a friend reading one or I might have heard about them on a TV book programme, or both! All I know is that I'm hooked and I can't wait until her next one comes out. My friends are the same. But I'm the one who buys them and then passes them on!

Speaker 2: It's the twists and turns in her plots that attract me to the books. They're certainly not straightforward and you can never guess the ending. I'm a bit of a crossword addict and I imagine that's why I like the books, they're real brain teasers. I don't think they come across at the cinema too well, though, although I suppose I have one of those versions to thank for getting me interested in the books in the first place! Whatever, they're definitely at the top of my list of the best books of all time. Much better than some of the books around now!

Speaker 3: I can't read one of her books without being reminded of my year studying in Paris. That was when I bought my first copy of her prize winning novel, *The Tower*. It was on our booklist for the course, but I didn't actually read it while I was in France because my French wasn't really good enough and you need to read her books in the original. So, I took it back to England with me and read it later. It definitely helped me get a better grade. I'm not sure which book is my favourite. I think it's probably that first one that I read. I'd definitely recommend her to anyone.

Speaker 4: I was going on holiday last summer and I needed a good book to read on the beach, so I had a good look round the bookshop at the airport. That's when I saw her latest novel. It was quite expensive, so I hesitated between getting that one and another detective story I'd seen advertised on TV. I must admit that I chose it because it just happened to be about the same town that I was going to. I'm glad I did get it. She's a terrific writer and I can't wait to see the film when it comes out next year.

Speaker 5: I had to spend some time in hospital earlier this year and I was getting totally fed up. I didn't want to do anything – read, crosswords, watch TV, nothing – especially not keep up with my schoolwork! It's difficult to get motivated about anything when you're in a hospital bed. My best mate knew how I was feeling and got me to read a novel by her favourite writer, a Swedish guy called Larsson. My favourite is usually fantasy novels and so I didn't think I'd like it much, but I loved it and couldn't put it down. Since then, I've seen the films they've made of the stories. Stunning! But not as good as the books.

Practice test Paper 3, Listening Part 4

Track 29

Interviewer: Today I'm talking to Zumba instructor, Vicky Baines. Vicky, what is Zumba and how did you become a teacher of it?

Vicky: Well, Zumba's a fitness craze that's taken over the world! It's a combination of aerobics and dance done to the music of South America. I went along to a class that my friend invited me to and I was hooked. I'm sure the fact that the teacher said I was a natural had something to do with it. I had no intention of teaching it at that point though, that was something that happened when I lost my job as a computer programmer and had to think of something else to do. I'd got tired of my boring office routine so when I saw a course advertised, I retrained and the rest is history!

Interviewer: So, how did Zumba become so popular so quickly?

Vicky: Well, I've got to admit that much as I love the exercise myself, the fact that it's become a craze worldwide is really unexpected. When I first started teaching, I had my doubts as to whether people would even come to the class – but I soon discovered that people are attracted to Zumba because it seems exciting. Though lots of people still prefer going to the gym or going for a run, Zumba attracts people who traditionally don't enjoy exercise.

Interviewer: Is it something that anyone can do, then?

Vicky: Absolutely, and I've got all kinds of people in my class, from young teens to pensioners. It's a great atmosphere, the music puts everyone in a great mood and they don't even realise they're working their bodies hard. I think more than anything people enjoy mixing with other people, much like they would at a party. Although you don't need a partner and while there are 'teach yourself' videos, it's not really something you could get much out of on your own in front of the TV.

Interviewer: How easy is it to achieve some level of success in Zumba?

Vicky: Well, like other dances, I do think it's helpful to be able to keep time with the music, but the routines aren't based on complicated movements like more traditional dance forms are. It doesn't matter if you have limited movement either – just come along and do what you can. You'll soon loosen your body up.

Interviewer: What do you like so much about teaching Zumba?

Vicky: The atmosphere is fantastic. I see a group of tired, ordinary people come along after work, change into their exercise clothes and come to life! I like to challenge my group by doing new combinations of the basic steps, though the moves are pretty much standard. The music is thrilling of course – no one could resist those Latin beats and I've bought some great compilations online.

Interviewer: What are the benefits of Zumba?

Vicky: Zumba's a great cardio-based workout that, not surprisingly, helps to tone and sculpt the body, so it's a great way to stay in shape as well as increase strength and coordination and, believe it or not, those are things that are beneficial for day to day activities too. But it works out more than your muscles. What I didn't realise when I started out is that it has a psychological benefit too and it really does wonders for your mood. People tell other people about how they feel and then they come and join the class too!

Interviewer: So, what are your plans for the future?

Vicky: Well, I've been asked to do a fitness video which I actually turned down because I don't like being in front of a camera. I've just started giving classes for kids, which is exciting, though the thing I'm really becoming passionate about is something called Aqua Zumba, which is done in a swimming pool. I've got a feeling that it will become even more popular than the dance form because exercising in water works your muscles even harder.

Practice test Paper 4, Speaking Part 1

Track 30

Interlocutor: First of all we'd like to know something about you.
Where are you from?
What do you like most about living there?
What sort of programmes do you enjoy watching on television? Why?
Where is your favourite place to spend a holiday? Why?

Practice test Paper 4, Speaking Part 2

Track 31

Interlocutor: In this part of the test, I'm going to give each of you two photographs. I'd like you to talk about your photographs on your own for about a minute and also to answer a short question about your partner's photographs.

Candidate A, it's your turn first. Here are your photographs. They show people learning in different ways. I'd like you to compare the photographs, and say what you think the advantages are of learning in these different ways.

All right?

Thank you.

Candidate B. Do you enjoy using a computer? Why or why not?

Candidate B, here are your photographs. They show people enjoying outdoor activities. Compare the pictures and say how you think the people are feeling.

All right?

Thank you.

Candidate A. Which activity would you prefer to do? Why?

Practice test Paper 4, Speaking Part 3

Track 32

Interlocutor: Now I'd like you to talk about something together for about two minutes.

Here are some ways that technology is changing people's lives today.

Talk together about how this technology is changing people's lives. All right?

You now have a minute to decide which is the most important change and why.

All right?

Practice test Paper 4, Speaking Part 4

Track 33

Interlocuter:

1 Some people say that it's impossible to live without a computer today. Do you agree? Why?

2 More and more young children are using mobile phones at an early age. Do you think this is a good thing? Why or why not?

3 Do you think children at primary schools should have technology lessons? Why or why not?

4 Do you think that advances in technology have made people in general much lazier? Why or why not?

5 Some people think that students should be allowed to use laptops in examinations. Do you think this would be a good thing?

6 Do you think technology can help us solve the world's problems? Why or why not?

Pearson Education Limited
Edinburgh Gate
Harlow
Essex CM20 2JE
England
and Associated Companies throughout the world.

www.pearsonELT.com

© Pearson Education Limited 2013

The right of Lynda Edwards and Helen Chilton to be identified as authors of this
Work has been asserted by them in accordance with the Copyright, Designs and
Patents Act 1988.

First published 2013
Third impression 2014

ISBN: 978-1-4479-0725-1 (Gold Pre-first Exam Maximiser with Key)

Set in Myriad Pro
Printed by Neografia in Slovakia

Acknowledgements

The publishers and authors would like to thank the following people and
institutions for their feedback and comments during the development of the
material:
Henrick Oprea, Atlantic Idiomas (Brazil), Sharon Gleave (Italy), Alan Del Castillo
(Mexico), Idiomas O'Clock team, Kamal K. Sirra (Spain), Jacky Newbrook (UK)

We are grateful to the following for permission to reproduce copyright material:

Text

Unit 2 Reading: adapted from www.guardian.co.uk/commentisfree/2008/
jun/06/antarctica.antarctica, Guardian News and Media Ltd; Unit 4 Reading:
adapted from http://www.guardian.co.uk/world/2011/jul/19/great-white-shark-
jumps-boat#start-of-comments, Guardian News and Media Ltd; Unit 5 Reading:
adapted from http://www.telegraph.co.uk/culture/3651694/Ive-swapped-my-
paper-clip-for-a-house....html, copyright (c) Telegraph Media Group Limited;
Unit 7 Reading: adapted from http://www.neatorama.com/2009/03/30/10-
craziest-diets-in-history/, Jill Harness/Neatorama.com; Unit 8 Reading: adapted
from http://www.guardian.co.uk/lifeandstyle/2009/jun/13/elephants-lawrence-
anthony-africa-family-life, Guardian News and Media Ltd; Practice Test
Reading Part 1: adapted from http://www.guardian.co.uk/travel/2006/mar/15/
culturaltrips.italy.venice?INTCMP=ILCNETTXT3487, Guardian News and Media
Ltd; Practice Test Reading Part 2: adapted from http://www.andycave.co.uk/
wp-content/themes/andycave/docs/RedBulletin_12_09.pdf http://issuu.com/
redbulletin.com/docs/1209_redbulletin_uk pp72-77 Nov 26/2009, The Red
Bulletin magazine

Photographs:
The publisher would like to thank the following for their kind permission to
reproduce their photographs:
(Key: b-bottom; c-centre; l-left; r-right; t-top)

Alamy Images: Aflo Foto Agency 71, Blue Tulip 69, Julian Brooks 22, Steve
Davey Photography 62, FancyVeerSet11 / Fancy 11, T. Grimm / vario images
GmbH & Co.KG 20 (C), IS638 / Image Source 46, LSC School / LatinStock
Collection 77r, Grantly Lynch / UK Stock Images Ltd 37cl, david pearson 28,
Picture Partners 95tr, Mike Powell / Corbis Flirt 40, Michael Prince / Corbis Flirt
20 (B), Scubazoo 37tr, Alex Segre 30, Michael Ventura 20 (A), funkyfood London
- Paul Williams 10, Andrew Woodley 37br, ZUMA Wire Service 19; **Bridgeman
Art Library Ltd:** Old Man Kangaroo at five in the afternoon, illustration from
'Just So Stories for Little Children' by Rudyard Kipling, 1951. Private Collection /
The Stapleton Collection 49; **Corbis:** Eureka Premium 77l, Patrik Giardino / Crush
67, James Hardy / PhotoAlto 34, Andrew Holbrooke / Corbis News 27t, Image
Source 42b, Tom & Dee Ann McCarthy / Cusp 55l, Erin Patrice O'Brien / Corbis
Entertainment 13b, Anna Peisl / Flirt 55r, Radius Images 42t, Eric Robert / Sygma
54; **Fotolia.com:** Boris Djuranovic 48, lizascotty 95br, Sorbotrol 95bl, tbcgfoto
33, Tobilander 13t; **Getty Images:** Brand X Pictures 23, Reza Estakhrian / Stone
39, Sue Flood / Oxford Scientific 37tl, Tim Hall / Photodisc 9, Marianna Massey
/ AFP 27b, Ray Mickshaw / FOX / Getty Images Entertainment 20 (D), Science
Photo Library 73, Michael Sewell / Peter Arnold 66, Michael Wong / Stockbyte
16; **Pearson Education Ltd:** Gareth Boden 95tl, Ian Wedgewood. Pearson
Education Ltd 20 (E); **Rex Features:** DAVID COLE 74, Alfred Weissenegger 25;
Shutterstock.com: 1000 Words 37bl, Dmytro Pylypenko 15, Olga Reutska 26,
travellight 64; **The Kobal Collection:** FOCUS FEATURES 57; **TopFoto:** Michael le
Poer Trench / ArenaPAL www.arenapal.com 61

All other images © Pearson Education

Every effort has been made to chase the copyright holders and we apologise
in advance for any unintentional omissions. We would be pleased to insert the
appropriate acknowledgement in any subsequent edition of this publication.

Illustrated by Oxford Designers & Illustrators